MY EXPERIMENTS WITH SILENCE

SAMIR SONI is an award-winning film, television and theatre actor. He was born and raised in Delhi. After finishing his schooling from St. Xavier's High School in Delhi, Samir moved to Los Angeles for higher studies. He graduated (cum laude) from the University of California, Los Angeles, in business economics. Samir went on to work as a financial analyst in mergers and acquisitions for Merrill Lynch. After two years on Wall Street, he decided to chuck everything and moved back to India to pursue his true passion, acting.

Over the last twenty-five years, he has won several awards and recognition for his work as actor in various mediums including web series. In 2018, he turned writer/director with his critically acclaimed debut film *My Birthday Song*, a psychological thriller, available on Netflix.

Samir has been very vocal about the importance of mental health and challenging the meaning of the word 'success' in society. He lives in Mumbai.

PRAISE FOR THE BOOK

'Going through Samir's experiments with silence reminds me of the scores of people fighting their inner demons. It's one thing to know your demons, it's quite another to actually face them squarely. Samir has had the courage to do both. I believe this book can help readers who want to get in touch with themselves but have been afraid to do so. This may just be the nudge they required.'

– Dr Varkha Chulani, clinical psychologist and psychotherapist

'An insight into the mind of an introvert ... a mind that's asking the right questions of identity and purpose, and taking us through his process of self-discovery. It takes courage to share snippets of one's personal diary, but this is evidence that writing is therapeutic, not only for the writer, but for the reader as well.'

– Sonali Bendre Behl, actor

'A sensitive and insightful take on life and finding your own path. Engaging and eloquent. A must-read for all generations.'

– Manjari Prabhu, author

'Samir writes from a place of genuine feeling. He bares his heart bravely, he mines its deepest (and sometimes darkest) corners to share an honest, thoughtful account of his roller-coaster life experiences.'

– Rajeev Masand, film critic

'It's wonderful to be able to express yourself, anxieties and all ... I'm sure this will echo the insecurities, fears, dreams and hopes of many and prove to be of great help.'

– Soha Ali Khan, actor and author

MY EXPERIMENTS WITH SILENCE

THE DIARY OF AN INTROVERT

SAMIR SONI

Om Books International

First published in 2021 by

Om Books International

Corporate & Editorial Office
A-12, Sector 64, Noida 201 301
Uttar Pradesh, India
Phone: +91 120 477 4100
Email: editorial@ombooks.com
Website: www.ombooksinternational.com

Sales Office
107, Ansari Road, Darya Ganj,
New Delhi 110 002, India
Phone: +91 11 4000 9000
Fax: +91 11 2327 8091
Email: sales@ombooks.com
Website: www.ombooks.com

ISBN: 978-93-91258-88-7

Printed in India

10 9 8 7 6 5 4 3 2 1

To all the misfit souls of the world,
living the inside out

prologue

The phase after the release of my not-so-successful first film and abrupt divorce was the most trying phase of my life. Nothing had prepared me for this double whammy. I had never hurt like this before and, worse still, I wasn't even sure why. I had experienced heartbreaks and failures before but it was never this bad. Determined not to ever feel like this again, I decided to confront my pain and not run away from it. Thus started my experiments with silence. The idea was to learn to be by myself, my pain, my fears, my disappointments and not to reach out for any distractions – phone, friends, TV or a book. The only luxury I allowed myself was writing. The following pages document my thoughts and emotions and revelations during this soul-searching experience which lasted almost two years, and is largely responsible for the man I'm today. It took me to places in my mind that I didn't even know existed and finally introduced me to the real me.

introduction

I was twenty-six years old and had taken the boldest decision of my life. After graduating (cum laude) from one of the top universities in business economics and a two-year stint on Wall Street as a financial analyst in a top investment bank, I decided to be a Bollywood film star. None of my family members or friends had anything remotely to do with Bollywood nor did I know a soul in Mumbai or had ever been there. But ever since I was eight years old and had attended my first acting workshop, I knew where I belonged. Being an introvert, the opportunity acting afforded me to be somebody else and let feelings out were therapeutic, and being appreciated for what others saw as a performance was the icing on the cake. Time passed, I continued with my passion and blossomed into an all-rounder, good in academics, sports and acting of course.

In college in Delhi, I decided to take mathematics as a subject, still focused on being an actor. Why mathematics? Well, it came a little easier and above all I was too damn lazy to read page after page of any other subject; it was too passive. Mathematics needed you to be alert, and once you understood the concept it was simple. In college, I continued to act in plays, became the cultural secretary of the college, studying enough to get by. But you can ride on two boats for only so long. Something has gotta give and it did. I failed in my second-year exams! A novel experience, a catastrophe. How could I show my face to anyone, friends, family? I was supposed to be the golden boy.

Almost thirty years later I still get nightmares about it, about not being prepared for a test, a scene, the clock is ticking but I can't remember the lines. Heart pounding, I'm dripping with sweat, please, God, help me, I'm drowning.

The next few years are a blur. All I remember is being shipped off to the US, studying with a vengeance in one of the top universities, getting my confidence back and landing this coveted job, almost trying to prove a point to myself and my family. Academics was a source of huge pride for my father because, growing up in a small town in Himachal Pradesh, he couldn't afford to finish school. He wanted to give his children the opportunities he never had. He and my mother pretty much sacrificed their entire life to give their sons the best education possible so that they could be 'somebody'. Regardless of what we sons have achieved, I don't think we can ever fill the dream in our parents' hearts, of being 'somebody'. My heart goes out to them and all those parents who sacrifice their lives for their children, thinking their children's 'success' will somehow ease the pain of not 'succeeding' in their life. I feel sorry for children who have to carry the crucifix of their parents' expectations. And I abhor this society which measures self-worth on the basis of how you walk, talk, live, drive and other such benchmarks. Many a people have lost their sanity or life living up to standards of the mighty few. It's all about being richer, bigger, faster, stronger, etc.

So here I was, working and living in Manhattan, getting paid the highest salary a college graduate could get in all of America and I was miserable. I didn't belong there and got no satisfaction from the job except the right to brag about working on Wall Street. It was films and acting that excited me. I believed I had what it takes to be a 'successful' actor and that I would be unable to live with myself for not having tried. So, I took the plunge. I quit my job on Wall Street and after some internal struggle and overcoming the fear of the unknown, with some money in the bank and a portfolio, I landed in Mumbai without a single plan in my mind.

After a series of up and downs, heartbreaks and disappointments, I found myself lying on a sofa in the living room of my two-bedroom apartment and staring at the moon. In one room were my parents and the other room my brother, all of whom had flown from Delhi to attend the premiere of my first film. Next day was a big day, probably the biggest day of my life. In the evening was the screening of my first film, with media, critics, special guests, followed by a major party attended by the who's who of Bollywood. The morning, however, was slightly different. I had to go to the marriage court to collect my final divorce papers.

Yes, within two years in Mumbai I had a whirlwind intense relationship which ended in a marriage within six months and a divorce in a year. As I lay on the sofa, a part of me was excited and nervous about the evening. What would it be like? Would the people like me? What should I wear? How and what should I say to the media? At the same time my heart was aching at the thought of the divorce. I didn't want it; surely, we could have worked things out, there were no major issues.

The next day my worst fears came true. The divorce did go through and the film, one of the biggest of the year, though critically appreciated, didn't do well at the box office. As far I was concerned, though reviews were favourable, most of my scenes were left out at the editing table. I had been rendered an invalid, with both my crutches taken away. My mind disoriented and heart bleeding, I fell down on the floor. And thus began my walk through the mist.

***

It's been almost a couple of decades now and I'm older and wiser. Well, definitely older. So, what have I learnt? As I look back, I realize that the point of the entire exercise was to explore pain, why certain things hurt so much and what I could do to ensure that it never happened again. To make myself immune to pain and disappointment. To thicken my skin, to fill all the chinks in my armour, so that everything would bounce off me. The journey took me to many places I wasn't ready to go, my childhood, my need to be wanted and at the same time resenting myself for wanting it because of the pain it was followed by when unfulfilled.

I realize, you are what you are by the age of five or six. After that you just develop coping methods to deal with this rather strange world, with your family, and extending it to the world at large. And that is the birth of your alter ego, which emerges whenever faced with a challenging situation. If these challenges are thrown at you incessantly, most (specially the introverts) develop one or more sub-personalities or just one dominant alter ego which protects the sensitive five-year-old child in you and faces the challenges on his behalf.

As time passes the wall between 'you' and your alter ego becomes unsurmountable, so much so that most people who 'know' you haven't really met the real you; even you for that matter associate yourself more with the alter ego and that's why you feel most relaxed when alone. Even when you're fifty years old, the part of you that laughs, cries, and gives you true joy and loves is still five, buried deep under scar tissues. As much as your alter ego protects the little child, it also suffocates it by not allowing it to express or experience.

It's a tough world if you are an introvert, because we live in an extroverted world. So, accept yourself for who you are, wear it as a badge of honour if you want. Don't try to conform to what you're not. You will fail. Be true to yourself and surround yourself with like-minded people, so there are no needs for the alter egos to exist.

For the longest time I thought there was something wrong with me. I'd be the only one watching Sachin Tendulkar play live in a stadium, with delirious screaming fans, and wished I was home alone in my pyjamas watching the same match on the TV with action replay. I thought I was strange when I felt more comfortable at a funeral than at a birthday party. I thought I was strange when after spending a lovely evening with my friends, I'd come home exhausted as if I had completed a major chore. I thought I was strange when at an award function I was almost relieved that I didn't win because I was going crazy thinking what I would say. I thought I was strange when I would get palpitations every time I had to go for a simple dinner (I would have to talk). I thought

I was strange when the need to make or receive a social call stressed me out. Maybe I was and still am crazy, or maybe I'm just your garden-variety ultra-sensitive introvert living in his head, trying to be or do the best that he can, fighting the value system of this extroverted world and still seeking the validation he was denied.

Just let me sleep tonight

Go away, you ghosts
Go away, you demons
Go and torment someone else tonight
For I have fought my fears
And I have shed my tears
And I just want to sleep tonight
Please let me sleep tonight

I don't care what happened
What could have
Or what still just might
I did what I had to do
And that is all there is to do

And I want to sleep tonight
Just let me sleep tonight

Go away, you God
Go away, you Devil
Go somewhere else
And fight your little fight
For I'm tired of being your pawn
Thinking I can still win
Whilst all is gone
And I just want to sleep tonight
Please let me sleep tonight

Come on, my little baby
Come on, my little angel
Come and tuck me in tonight
For I have fought my fears
And I have shed my tears
And I just want to sleep tonight
Please help me sleep tonight

1

Need peace, which only writing seems to provide.
Alone with one's own thoughts. A crutch similar
to another person's company, but only more
effective for it lightens one's mind without
making the soul hollow. It resolves issues,
leaving one stronger and more in control, and
not weak and a slave of one's urges. **Thank
God** for it and apologies for looking for the
easier way out. Perhaps it's a good idea to
write every day, rather every night, or whenever
one needs to. It's quite difficult to live by
one's standards if they are too high. But it
does feel good when one can. All analysis is
meaningless! One can think and plan all one
wants but when the moment of truth comes, it's
one's character that takes one through. Character
is what we are made of, and that cannot be
changed. One **hopes and prays** that when the
test comes, one's character lives up to one's
expectations. **Perhaps no!** True character cannot

be changed. Do feel a little sleepy, a sure sign
of peace. Hope.

Shhh, quiet!
Silence inside and
outside. Silence!

2

Not really feeling different, perhaps a little paralysed. Instead of fighting this state of inactivity, trying to come to terms with it and accepting it. Unlike other moments when writing **clears the mind**, it is making things worse. It's showing me the mirror. Nothing really to say or write — only to do. Need peace, a little nap. Just have to clear my mind and all is going to be fine. Sooner or later have to take the leap, the sooner the better. Just have to get set and go! Have to, have to, have to!

3

Lull after the storm. All is **quiet** ... inside and outside. I thank **God** for it. But, where do we go from here? THE PEACE IS ADDICTIVE AND HYPNOTIZING. The stillness is soothing if felt and eerie if thought about.

4

28 January

Writing after a **long time** ... at least it feels that way. Spending too much time thinking. Always land up depressing myself further. Have to resolve the issue and start getting ready. Feel quite tired and burnt out. Not quite clear how to get out of it. It's been weeks since I felt full of energy and motivated. Seem to be having an identity crisis WHO AM I? WHAT DO I WANT? Or maybe I just don't like the reality that I'm being forced to face. Have to stop running.

5

EVENTFUL MORNING, reminded once again of a lesson. Silence is golden. Do not talk about people, nothing good ever comes out of it. There are no secrets. What goes around comes around. You reap what you sow. You will pay ... always ... eventually. There is no getting away. **STAY AWAY, STAY CLEAR.** There is no black or white, only shades of grey. But trying to keep your clothes clean does not mean taking no stand. Try to resolve the issues without pointing fingers, for you do not know the complete picture. If you're unable to resolve, just be an unbiased listener. Do not get sucked in and worsen the issue.

'Nothing is sometimes a good thing to do and always a good thing to say.'

2 February

PAYING THE PRICE FOR INDULGENCE. Got stuck in front of the TV for too long. Watched it even though the fun of it was long gone. Just trying to escape from reality. **What stops me?** There really isn't much to it, yet one mulls over it endlessly. Just waiting for the moment when everything will be just right. One waits and waits but something or the other is always wrong. Until one can't take it any more, and finally all the analyses are thrown out of the window and the leap of faith is taken. **BE CALM.**

7

Things are not very difficult. **Restless, tired, uneasy, anxious.** Looking for a silver lining. Clarity. Anxiety before the leap, like the day before the exam. Need a short nap, a little escape to recharge.

Lost Soul

LOST SOUL, LOST SOUL, LOST SOUL I AM
Don't know where I've been or where I'm going
Don't even know who the hell I am
Fed up of myself, fed up of my being, fed up of everything I see
Just fed up, fed up, fed up of everything and anything about me.
YES, LOST SOUL, LOST SOUL, LOST SOUL I AM
Don't know where I've been or where I'm going
Don't even know who the hell I am

BOY! Think I'm having an anxiety attack again. Going through millions of emotions. Finding it very difficult to focus. Wonder why. What is this anxiety all about? I **GUESS** there are too many unanswered questions. But everything works out in the end and there really isn't any reason to worry. **Just have to take one step at a time.**

Desperately seeking myself. WHO AM I? WHERE DO I LIVE? WHAT DO I LOOK LIKE? WHAT DO I WANT? DOES ANYONE CARE? SHOULD ANYONE CARE? Am I a self-obsessed dreaming loser who doesn't know what he wants or how to get it? Or simply too lazy to make the effort? Where are you? What are you hiding from? **And what are you waiting for?**

10

Don't feel too great. Tired and fed up. I hope I get the job. Don't want to dump my insecurities on other people, and **I WON'T!** I want to be good, not bad. I probably won't get the job because there are many others who are more suitable, but hope I deserve it more. A little bit of help from **God** will go a long way. **But I've never given up.** Didn't give up when I was in school, didn't give up in college, and am certainly not going to give up now. **If more effort is what is needed, more effort is what I'm going to give. No retreat, no surrender!**

11

18 February

FEEL QUITE THE SAME. Looking for light at the end of the tunnel. LOOKING FOR A LITTLE BIT OF GOD'S MERCY. Is it a losing battle? Are my passion and my principles my enemies?

Is that what is holding me back?

12

JUST HAD A FLASH FROM MY PAST. Eerie ... wonder if one should dwell on it. One makes choices and sometimes when one sits and thinks of the price paid, things look scary. The only way to chase the rainbow is to ignore how far it is. But when one snaps out of this MADNESS MOMENTARILY, one realizes how far one has come and how much one has sacrificed. But the morning comes and it's time to take yet another step towards the zenith. **One just hopes and prays that one is on the right path.**

My First Literary Piece

I was seven years old, shy and awkward, and had this huge crush on my cousin who was about eight or nine years older. She was also quite fond of me. Every summer I used to look forward to her visiting us in Delhi. I don't recall spending any special moments with her but, growing up in an all-boys family, in my mind she was the sister I never had and desperately wanted. But this summer things were a little different. I found myself being ignored by her. My eldest brother, who was closer to her age, wasn't keeping well, and naturally she was spending more time with him. At least that's what I remember. Also, she had been in the house for a little over two days and what on earth would a seventeen-year-old girl have to share with a seven-year-old kid? But reason had no place in my hypersensitive heart. I sulked for a couple of days and when I couldn't take it any more, I decided to take some action. I wrote a little note to her and put it in her handbag, where she could not miss finding it. I distinctly remember the note. It had four or five lines, 'you don't love me', 'you don't talk to me', 'you have changed', etc., each sentence ending with a capital 'WHY?'.

I waited for the next morning anxiously. I'm not quite sure what I was expecting when I went to sleep that night but nothing could have prepared me for what was about to come. I remember waking up to murmurs and giggles outside my room. This was not a good sign. Then I heard the loud sound of my brothers laughing and my mom asking questions incredulously. *'Oh my God! What have I done!'* I thought to myself in extreme embarrassment. *'I'm never going to hear the end of this.'* I lay there in my bed, motionless, eyes tight shut, my heart pounding. *'What do I do now? How long can I pretend to be sleeping?'* I could feel a piece of paper in my hands but could not muster the courage to read it. After about ten minutes, which actually felt like an hour, I rushed into the washroom with the piece of paper in my hand. It was the same note that I had written, with some sweet words from my sister and a glaring mistake with a little red circle around it. I had spelled 'Why' as 'WAY', four times, at the end of each sentence and in bold. Oh, how I wished the earth would open and swallow me. Spending the rest of my life in a washroom wasn't an option. So, slowly I opened the door and walked out as normally as I could without making any eye contact. The rest of the day was a blur, some kind smiles, some giggles with an exclamation from my mom, 'What! You don't know how to spell "why?".' I was crushed. I don't know if I was more heartbroken or embarrassed. It had taken a great deal of courage to write that note and I had made an utter fool of myself.

Somewhere around that time the seed of a 'lesson' was sowed, a lesson that, over the years, was reinforced again and again, and that shaped the person I am today. Never depend on other people for emotional needs. Not only you risk not getting what you need, but you also risk being humiliated. And even if you truly need it, never ever show it. Since then, I've had a love-hate relationship with validation. I need it, but hate myself for needing it. I have actively worked on this 'weakness' and have somewhat succeeded by looking more and more inward and practising detachment.

13

Peaceful! All is **Quiet** for now, but things are far from settled. Got miles to go before sleep ... miles to go. **Thank you, God, just be with me.**

14

Not much to do. Watched TV all day long. No deep introspective thoughts, just killing time. Even when one makes a conscious effort to probe, the mind gets flooded with worries about work. Let's hope tomorrow brings some good news. All is okay, no problems as such. Just have to play the waiting game. It's 7.45 p.m. GUESS I'll get something to eat. The weather outside looks pretty good. It was raining sometime back, but it seems to have stopped now. It is still cool and cloudy. Sure would love to take a walk, but can't trust the weather. As much as I'm enjoying this, it's time to get going. Later alligator.

15

28 February

STRESSED, unable to relax. Tried watching TV, reading ··· but nothing helped. Hope this helps; it's the last resort. ANXIETY, along with the fear of FAILURE and making MISTAKES, is really killing. Need to pull myself together or else I'll just go nuts. Need to focus and get my priorities right.

16

Just faced a setback. It was minor, but hurts bad.
GUESS NOBODY said life was going to be easy. It
wasn't the first and definitely will not be the
last. **ANYWAY**, HAVE NOT GIVEN UP SO FAR, and will not
give up now. Just have to keep my head down
and keep working away. Have no control over
the outcome. Have to be the
best that I can be. **GOD WILL
TAKE CARE
OF THE REST.**

17

2 March

It's 6.45 in the morning.

COULDN'T GET SLEEP ALL NIGHT. SERVES ME RIGHT!
I deserve every bit of it. FED UP! Live and
learn, I **GUESS**. Only that I don't know what I've
learnt. Not to open up to people and expose
myself? Who knows and who cares? At least,
I'm up early in the morning. No matter what, **my
world is okay.** People are nice and I trust
them. Whatever will be, will be, the future's not
ours to see.

18

Got nothing to say. Must **I always** ... Is God watching? Perhaps he is watching, and therefore ... **Plans, strategies** ... but even no strategy is yet another strategy. It is indeed peaceful to be alone with one's own thoughts. Seems to give focus. Have failed before and will fail again. **GUESS**, pain is good, for it gives you motivation. Nice to be sad and alone, far and away from the outside. Down but not out. Just licking my wounds, but **I'll be back.** There is no other way to go. Whenever one goes outside, all one hears is: **'YOU CAN'T.'** But the moment you retreat deep within yourself, the same old familiar voice takes over. The voice you've heard ever since you were a child: 'You're special, you can, you can, and sooner or later you will, and you know it. So stop crying about what is not and get on with what you've got.' Yes, I will do it. But must it be so difficult? **GUESS**, in the struggle lies the fun, especially when deep down you know, you will, you will, you will!

19

6 March

Sunday morning. being alone was eating me up. The urge to pick up the phone and ... anything but be alone. Waiting anxiously for the phone to ring. BUT IT'S OKAY NOW. I **GUESS** if you hold on long enough, things settle down. Have to accept the bad with the good for the choices one makes. But we're all right for now. One hopes and wishes that things would have worked out differently or were like they used to be. But that was then, and this is now.

Don't Know ... Thank you. GOD .

20

7 March

Have been living from day to day for so long that it feels strange to take stock of the situation. It's like meeting an old friend after a very long time. One doesn't know where to start. Still suffering from the todays, yesterdays and the tomorrows. The past few months have been such a roller-coaster that it's difficult to get a perspective, let alone come to terms with it. Everything is a blur. But feels nice to be able to step aside, even if only for a moment. Not recovering from what you did or did not, not preparing for what you will or will not. Just being. Used to be a lot easier but it has been a trifle difficult of late. So has rising above the daily pettiness that a busier and more interactive life breeds. I **GUESS**, 'It's hard to be a saint in A CITY.' But all said, written and done, it's 1996, and I'm still around and not doing too terribly.

25

Sure would be interesting to know where life takes me from here ... to heaven or hell, only time will tell. Probably to heaven through hell. Ha! Sure hope it's not the other way around. What if it does happen that way? What if now *is* heaven and it's only hell waiting for me? I can sense my Ol' friend fear creeping in. Boy! Fear sure can freak you out sometimes. **GUESS** I'm back to where I started, recovering from yesterday, worrying about tomorrow and as far as 'stepping aside and just being' is concerned, I **GUESS** some other day, some other time.

Living

Living by the scripture – whatever that means
Looking for happiness or what it seems
A silver lining, a little escape
A few short breaths of the fresh air I take
To be alive, to be free
Free from what was or wasn't
Free and alive in the 'now', the present.
To be in the middle of it, in the thick of action
To fight, but no! not with passion
May be passion is what I need
Something is wrong, something amiss
SOMETHING I DIDN'T REMEMBER, SOMETHING I JUST MISSED
What? Where, when and how?
No, I must **WAKE UP** now.
WAKE UP and smell the sweet fresh air
The little red rising sun with its glory everywhere
Alive and free in the 'now', the present
Let others worry about what was or wasn't.

21

10 March

It's a beautiful afternoon. A lot of activity outside ... **BIRDS FLYING**, trees swaying, even the sea seems in a **high tide** ... With the sound of the sea waves one can hear the voice of kids playing cricket on the beach. Quite pretty. Life doesn't seem too terrible either. CONTENT, AT LEAST FOR THE TIME BEING WITH THE WAY THINGS ARE SHAPING UP. See some light at the end of the tunnel. Looks like we are on the right track, and we're alright for now.

22

Waiting to fall asleep. The longer it takes, the more ANXIOUS one gets, the more CONSCIOUS one gets, the longer it takes. Wanted to write, but the thoughts are clouded with ANXIETY. Tomorrow is yet another test, still feels like the first. Success is SCARY. One wants to share it and enjoy it, and yet is SCARED that someone or something will take it away. Also, sharing at times feels like bragging or showing off, both telltale signs of INSECURITY at best and shallowness/immaturity at WORST. After all, shouldn't a work well done in itself be satisfying? Must one seek approval or appreciation to feel good? Especially since it doesn't really make one feel good and leaves one feeling so small. Yet, when the moment arises one becomes a slave of one's insecurities and does what one abhors the most. One is left feeling feeble and helpless like a little kid who would do or sell anything to be accepted, even if what is so dear to him, such as his pride, is at stake. Have to stop. Have to fight this slavery of urges and insecurities. It's not difficult; have to have faith in oneself and one's abilities. Faith, confidence, TRUST, BELIEF!

My First 'This Is It' Moment

Growing up in the late 1970s, the Oscars, rather the award ceremonies of the Oscars, had a great impact on me. I would sit in front of our black-and-white TV and absorb all the speeches given by these tuxedo-clad people. I don't think I knew who they were but the look in their eyes and the glorious words they spoke, thanking everyone, especially their wife, with the black trophy in their hand mesmerized me. I would spend hours in front of a mirror with a bottle of water in my hand, giving my own version of their speech. The peculiar thing was I always thanked my non-existent 'wife'. Being a die-hard romantic, I found that very touching. I always looked forward to getting married, winning an award, giving a profound and entertaining speech and of course thanking my wife. As luck would have it, the very first TV serial I did after coming back from the US gave me my first (there were more to come) 'this is it' moment. The entire cast of our show was going to be felicitated at an annual function of an organization. The show hadn't even been aired but the makers saw this as a good opportunity to get some publicity and the organizers thought the audience would find it entertaining. So, there I was in a hall full of people ready to give my much-rehearsed speech.

One by one our names were called, there was a thunderous applause and a cast member would receive the trophy, say a few words and gracefully step down from the stage. My turn was just round the corner and I was super excited, wearing my black-pin striped Armani suit, a shirt and a tie. Finally, the anchor announced, 'Next to receive his trophy the debutant, SAMIR SONI!' I took a deep breath and got up from my seat but one thing was different. There was no applause, not even a token clap. One would have thought they had announced a two-minute silence as a mark of respect for the passing away of some luminary.

Those fifteen to twenty steps to the centre of the stage felt like going to the gallows. I thought to myself, *hey I'm new, they don't know who I'm yet*, and proceeded to receive the trophy and start my speech. 'Ladies and gentleman, it gives me great pleasure to...' Pin-drop silence. I could feel droplets of sweat around my collar. I was starting to stutter now. And then it happened. A loud booming voice from the balcony, '*Abey angrez, Hindi mein bol*'. The entire hall broke into roaring laughter and among them were six of my own family members, hiding their faces. I ran off the stage. Later when I confronted my family for not clapping, my brother said, in his own unique Delhi style, '*Yaar main taali bajane wala tha, phir itna silence ho gaya ki lagaa ki taali bajai toh hummein padegi.'* (I was about to clap, brother. And then it became so silent that I felt I would be thrashed if I clapped.)

Thus ended my first 'this is it' moment. And there were more to come.

23

Where do we go FROM HERE? Got lots to do. Didn't sleep too well last night. DRUGGED, but we are all right for now. Drinking **COFFEE**, listening to music, **watching the sunset**. Hope He's watching too. Be true to yourself and the stream will find its way.

24

Quite an eventful day. Had a glimpse of the Promised Land as well as the rock bottom of my own FEARS. The waters were quite **turbulent** today, but we survived yet again, as we should have, for the storm was only one's own mind and the water was actually quite still. But who knows **what lies beneath the calm, still surface?** But if the ship is strong and the captain able, the rest is just a matter of passing through. Unfortunately, at times the ship is a LITTLE WEAK, the captain a little unsure, and the waters a LITTLE ROUGH. Hell breaks loose and heaven nowhere to be seen. And then ... hush ... Quiet. Let it be. Let it be.

25

It's only 12.45 in the afternoon, and my eyelids are already feeling heavy. Thought of an old friend crossed my mind. Looked for similarities and hoped not to find any. Sleep is just an escape. There are ups and downs in life. **THINGS PLAY WITH YOUR MIND AND HEART.** One tries to intellectualize away every move to prevent it from rocking the boat, but in the process one loses the excitement of the struggle. So powerful is the mind that it manages to take away the sting from failure but not without taking away the excitement from success. BUT ISN'T THAT THE WAY ONE OUGHT TO BE? To be able to see success and failure alike. But then what is life if not success and failure, joy and sorrow. Take all that away and what is one left with? A detached existence without passion or prejudice. Perhaps, that is what life is ...**strife** to reach a stage of detachment. To do your duty and not worry about results. To do your job and let God do his. Amen!

26

BOY! The mind is in such a mess. The highs and the lows, one worse than the other. The lows are bad, the highs - if one can call them so - are even worse. Swaying like a yo-yo from despair to FRUSTRATION ... Despair at being no good, the frustration of being so good, **yet** ... Everything seems to be driven by the result, the desire for success and the fear of failure. The key is to find PEACE WITHIN YOURSELF. To discover your own identity, the essence of your being and be true to it, and not get swayed by everything that comes your way. Internal peace is what one needs to keep in touch with oneself, and the rest will follow.

Things We Do, Things We Say

THINGS WE DO, THINGS WE SAY
Things we mean to, things we convey
WHO'S WRONG? WHO'S RIGHT?
A little misunderstanding, a little oversight
WHO SAID WHAT? WHERE? WHEN? AND WHY?
Who cried silently, who didn't bat an eye

At the end of the day

Aren't we all a little tired and a little dead?

Wondering about the things we did and things we said.

27

FEEL WEAK, HOLLOW, EMPTY AND SOULLESS. Unable to take decisions alone. Then the desire to be respected and appreciated. Everything is for sale … one's truest feelings … deepest fears most personal experience, everything … All for a little compassion, for that little glint of acceptance and admiration. NOTHING IS SACRED, EVERYTHING IS THERE JUST TO BE USED SOMEDAY, SOMETIMES FOR MOMENTARY SATISFACTION.

28

Another day of indulgence and yet another day of slavery. Slave to one's habits and urges. A bundle of WEAKNESSES and SHORTCOMINGS. Spoke too much, spoke trash and acted like one. To be accepted, to fit in and to be liked, just talk, talk and talk ... HAVE TO LEARN, HAVE TO STAY AWAY, HAVE TO SHUT UP.

29

GRACE UNDER PRESSURE. Waiting for immunity, airtight, crack-proof! In discipline lies the freedom, **God Knows** ... that is, if he is watching. **Shhh... Talk too much!** Have to shut up. **Quiet!** Don't let anyone rock the boat – friends, family or foes. Nobody. *NOBODY MATTERS.* It's just you and GOD AND THE REST IS JUST BY THE WAY, INCIDENTAL, INCONSEQUENTIAL. Your world begins and ends with you, for in you is God. So don't cheapen him by selling him. Deliver me from evil.

30

NOT MUCH TO WRITE, NOT MUCH TO SAY. Need peace, not indolence or laziness but peace, alertness and focus. Peace is not and should not mean **disillusionment from reality**, better recognized as the tangible and materialistic **WORLD**. Indeed, peace is the realization of the true nature of this **ever-changing world** and then working within its parameters. For, tranquility is NOT POSSIBLE by being oblivious of the present or simply ignoring it and merely contemplating the beyond or the ideal state. It is achieved by doing one's duties without passion or prejudice within **this materialistic world**.

Summer of 1980

As far back as I can remember, I always sat in the extreme corner of the classroom, if not the last bench, the second-last one. It was my comfort zone, closest to the exit door, hidden by my three best mates, two in the front and one next to me. Also, it gave me a bird's-eye view of the entire classroom. Four of us always had our own session of jokes and notes being passed around, all along keeping out of the line of vision of the teacher. Avoiding the teacher's gaze in itself was a great game, ducking and weaving behind the students in front of us. It was even funnier if one of us was called out by the teacher, watching the poor chap squirm, trying to make sense of what was written on the blackboard or the last words he could remember coming out the teacher's mouth, trying hard to keep a straight face watching his misery.

By now I had blossomed from a timid, introverted, shy kid to this confident, cool hero of the class if not the entire school. This was largely because of my exploits on stage and sports that gave me the confidence. The students loved me, for I always stood up for them, and the teachers liked my cheekiness because I was decent in academics as well. I was a guy's guy. Despite being in an all-boys school, I had somehow developed this reputation of being popular with the girls in every interschool competition I went to. Little did anyone know that I was petrified of being alone with a girl. Growing up in an all-boys family, being the youngest of three brothers, going to an all-boys school, girls were strange creatures you could only hide from and admire from a distance.

When it came to the telephone it was altogether a different ball game. I was the king. I would chat for hours on the phone. I had no idea who the girl was … just listening to a sweet voice and my imagination had no bounds. There was snow all around, a log cabin, a fireplace, a guitar in my hand whispering sweet nothings. Even Mr Yash Chopra would have a lot of catching up to do. I was in love. Every now and then a different girl would call, and I would be in love with her too. Sometimes the same girl would call using a different name and I would be in love with both. I guess I was in love with being in love, it was such a beautiful escape, and their responses made me feel good about myself. I would always get that warm fuzzy feeling when I finally put the phone down.

Well, I was fourteen and just believing that I 'loved' someone and that person 'loved' me back was enough. I didn't care who she was or what she looked like. All that was important was how it made me feel. Besides, knowing who or what she looked like would require meeting (these were pre-mobile days) and that was an alternative reality of which I had no experience and which I dreaded. But I do recall meeting one of my phone amores. It was our annual school festival, the only day girls were allowed in the school campus. There I was wearing my dark-tinted spectacles, looking absolutely idiotic as the sun had set and it was already dark. I had my pointed boots on, with slightly flared trousers, Tony Monero would have been proud of me. And there she was wearing a pink dress, ribbon in her long hair, looking as nervous as me. We took a few rounds of the fair, chaperoned by her college-going elder sister, exchanged maybe ten or fifteen words amid sneaking glances at each other and the people around. After about an hour of awkwardness we bid each other goodbye and I exhaled.

That was my first 'date', if you could call it one. First date among the handful I might have had in my lifetime. For fear of rejection or just general awkwardness, I've almost never asked anyone out for a date and stayed in the friend zone. Anyway, by next day, it had spread like wildfire. 'Samir came with a girl to the school festival.' I was a bona fide 'star', with almost everyone, including some seniors, coming to me asking if I could introduce them to so and so girl. Little did they know that this star was actually a damp cracker on a Diwali night. But I just smiled and soaked it all in, and that was the summer of 1980.

31

Quite an eerie night, not very different from the night before. It's Quiet and I'm alone. I GUESS there's something about nights like these, cold out of season, that makes you feel this way. Just hate being alone. Feel a little SCARED, like in those horror films. But feeling better since I've started writing. Thoughts seem to wander all over the place. Seem to constantly oscillate between the past, present and future. It's amazing how even before one has barely started thinking about 'what will', one is brought back to 'what did' or 'what could have' and how quickly that changes the complexion of 'what will'. Insecurities, insecurities, insecurities ... guess that's what life is all about, thousands of small battles day after day and not just one big one. But...

32

LYING ALL ALONE WITH MY THOUGHTS. It's unseasonably cold but I'm warm. The evening is setting in, the table lamp is on and I am lost. Things are building up, don't know how long the dam will hold before the waters break loose. It's getting increasingly difficult to write. FEAR of INTERPRETATIONS and writing for someone other than myself make it seem all too pretentious. SCARED of losing, even tears seem poor consolation as I'm not the only one. Haunted by the ghosts, they just don't seem to leave me alone. Losing fast, but have to face them or else soon they'll devour me. Ashamed of myself for not being able to rise to my own strength and too proud to ask for help. Tears seem meaningless; hurt seems meaningless, even words seem meaningless. Lost, need help but nobody else can. Have to fight my demons myself.

33

THERE HE SAT ALONE, THINKING. In a state of daze, going over the past for the zillionth time. There was a sense of loss and a fear of the loss being permanent. Perhaps if he accepted the present he could move on. He wanted to cry but no tears would come, only **CONVULSIONS.** He sat there waiting for the storm to blow over, wondering what *GOD HAD IN STORE FOR HIM. THERE REALLY WAS NO WAY OUT BUT TO WEATHER THE STORM.* It was time to conserve until a better tomorrow and just wait for the sun to rise again. For he knew that the sun would rise and the dark clouds would pass. **But at the moment nothing made sense, except to go deep inside the silence between thoughts where no one could touch him until it was time to come out again.**

Only the Brave

And there he rose yet again
Through all the misery and all the pain
Not with anger but with a smile
For he knew all he had to do is just wait a while
And tomorrow would be another day
Full of happiness and God's mercy everywhere
But tonight, he has to reach deep inside
And muster all the strength
that he can find
Far and away from friends, family and foe
Deep, deep within himself where only the blessed go.

34

Brain is all messed-up. Self-esteem really down. ANXIOUS, RESTLESS, no peace at all. Not even clarity. The only comfort is the belief good times will come. Cannot humiliate myself any further. Just hope the day comes soon. Until then one has to just wait and be patient. **Before** you know it, the bad times will pass. Just have to be patient and wait. Just ride the storm and the waters will be calm soon. Don't worry. it will pass ... whatever it is. Just dont humiliate yourself any further. gain strength and lie low, it will pass.

35

Comfortably numb. Everything seems to be driven by fears. Fear of loss, fear of failure, fear of being laughed at. Although I know that fears are only ghosts from my childhood that have come to haunt me again. But their hold is stifling. THE ONLY WAY OUT IS TO FACE THEM. For there is no greater sin in the world than to fear. Have to stop protecting **the little boy**. Have to let him face his fears and conquer them. It is only then he will grow up and it's only then I will be complete.

Music of the Night

As far as I can remember I always loved nights, just being able to be alone with my thoughts, dreaming and gently drifting while everyone in the house was fast sleep. At night, time stood still, no hustle-bustle of the day, nothing to do and nowhere to be. Even the streets were all empty with no noise. Apart from a bark or two from the stray dogs chasing an isolated car, there was complete silence. If you stood still for a moment, you could actually hear the sound of the breeze. It was a different time, a different world and Mother Nature seemed to be at peace with the universe.

I always slept with my window open so I could see and hear the trees gently sway in the summer breeze and the moonlight filtering through. I've always had an unusual fixation for the moon. It always represented the face of God smiling from above. I didn't grow up in a very religious family, but 'God' had a very important role to play in my life. He saw everything, knew everything and justice would always be done. He was the father figure who always stood by me and told me to do the right thing. At night He and I would have our conversations. I would stare at Him and he would stare back at me with a smile and tell me, 'Don't worry, everything will be okay' and I would drift off to sleep, a smile on my face, wrapped in the cosy moonlight beam.

I clearly remember, after a rough day at school, having this conversation with Him, 'You don't fool me, God. I know I'm your favourite son. You throw me in the ocean but just when I'm about to drown you will pick me up, for you know that I don't know how to swim. You will never let me drown, but just when I get too comfortable, you'll throw me right back into the ocean. It's not because you're mean, it's because you want me to learn how to swim. I will learn, my lord, I will learn but I'm not afraid any more.' Simple words of a simple child, trying to make sense of the world he lived in.

Those were indeed simple days, at least as I look back now. We would have our dinner by 7:30 p.m. Then everyone in the lane would go for evening walks, elders in one group and children behind them in another. There was no fear of being run over by a car or suffocating pollution. The air was clean, traffic well under control and 'outside' was a good and safe place to be. There we were in our kurta pajamas, parents discussing politics and we kids sharing some or the other story. It was, at least seemed, wholesome and innocent. Yes, we didn't have mobiles, iPads, colour TVs, or even air conditioning.

And power shortage was a normal thing at nights. So you could be fast asleep at twelve in the night, and suddenly the sound of the water cooler or the fan would come to a grinding halt. Soon all the neighbours would gather together at the electricity box and wait for the local municipality electrician to come and fix the problem. Annoying as it was, it was also kind of funny watching the elders fret and fume over the working of the local government. On days when we were informed in advance that there would be no electricity at night, everyone made their own arrangements. Some moved their folding beds to the terrace and others, like us, moved our beds to our front lawn. And just in case it got too hot, we would sprinkle our cotton mattresses with some water and go off to sleep before it dried. Those were the 'good ol' days', we didn't have much but felt happier than with all we have today.

Under the starry night
And the moon shining bright
Peacefully we all slept
Not a worry on our mind
Or what tomorrow we might find
Tonight we all slept as one
Happily, until the morning sun.

36

NOISES. LOUD NOISES, NO CLARITY, NO BLACKS,
WHITES OR GREYS, INSTEAD A ZILLION COLOURS,
ALL SPLASHED TOGETHER, CLASHING AND
JARRING. Not even a resemblance of any order.
Complete mayhem. Every noise is driven by
goddamn fear and is self-inflicted. Fucking
bullshit fear, nothing else but fear. Fear of this,
fear of that. What if this? What if that? Hate it!
Only illusions, no reality whatsoever. You
believe the illusion and thus the pain and the
anger. And what is there to fear? Loss? Isn't that
the best way to ensure the loss? By being afraid
of it occurring. Just be, leave it to God. What
will be will be. Don't be so arrogant as to try
and play God by trying to plan the future. That's
all bullshit. Destiny is what will be, for God acts
through you. He knows what your deepest driving
desire is, and that is your destiny. You yourself

56

might not realize what it is that you want, but God does. The stream always has and always will find its way. Can't go wrong for there is no right or wrong, only God acting through you for your ultimate good. **All's well, no noise, no fear, only silence, beautiful lovely silence. At peace, finally.**

37

What is, what could have been and what will be. Plagued by questions. Not quite sure what I want or even what I'm hoping for. Maybe I do, but just don't want to accept it. Just waiting for destiny to hand me my cards. Haunted by the past and SCARED about the future. But the fear seems to be diminishing, perhaps because of the realization that whatever happens, happens for the best. Time will take its course no matter what. To hope that my future, by **God's grace, is bright and happy.** There's no point struggling. Have done all I could, the rest is in God's hands. Still appallingly attached to the memories. Perhaps now the memories have become a crutch. **GUESS**, when things are rough, it's better to just lie low. Have to have confidence and faith in myself and what I believe in and the rest is God's will. And I will accept it for better or worse; for I don't know any better. Until then, I'll just wait.

38

10 April

ALONE, LONELY AND SAD. But not out. There are no
solutions. Only time has the answers. One can
do nothing but wait and pray to God for
deliverance. It's just a matter of time and
everything will be all right. Hanging on to the
past desperately. WAITING FOR GOD, for His is the
glory, the world and everything in it. Like I
said, alone, lonely and sad but certainly not out,
for I know God is with me and as long as He is,
nothing can go wrong. I know I shall find my
own peace of mind for I have been promised a
place of my own. Inshallah!

39

Spent the day where I belong, deep within myself. Still felt the occasional jitters but feeling better than before. By and large leaving things to God, taking each day as it comes. What has to happen will happen, circumstances evolve in such a way that the inevitable does actually happen. Have to maintain my peace, although even that is taken care of by God. Just have to walk in faith and sooner or later everything will be all right. As much we would like to believe otherwise, there really isn't too much in our hands. But there isn't any need to worry for God has better plans. All one has to do is watch life unfold in front of our eyes and take the rough with the smooth. **GUESS**, I'll just have to lie low, conserve energy and ride the rough with the smooth. Hope tomorrow is just as peaceful as today. Thank you, God, for everything and above all for my peace of mind. Thank you.

40

And thus life rolls on. The sun rises, the sun
sets, night comes and then it's time for the sun
to rise again. Life goes on and on, through all
the misery and pain, through all the fears and
uncertainty. Life just keeps on going as it well
should. For this is the only way good times
come. But there is momentary peace in despair.
There is stillness in the journey when one is not
so impatiently waiting for it to end. The rain
and dark cloud also have their warmth, the sun
and the barren deserts also have their moments
of coolness. Why not enjoy the misery when one
knows it's only temporary? It's been a long, long
drought and the clouds are nowhere near. Well, I
guess until they come, I will just have to enjoy
the dry sun and thank God for these moments
of clarity.

41

Too much of internal dialogue, too much noise, not enough silence between thoughts. A constant barrage of questions. **Why did I? Why couldn't I? Why? Why? Why** ... and even before a question can be answered, another one is just waiting to pounce at me. **ENDLESS**, pointless, senseless debate. And it is stupid to expect others to **ANSWER MY QUESTIONS** because they do not know where I am, where I've been or where I am going to. Besides, everyone has their own problems, their own experiences and thus their own twists to the story. **Truly pointless. So where does that leave me?** Alone, with all my anxieties, all my problems and only me to solve them. Lucky me, for I've got the best person for the job.

42

EARLY MORNING AND ALL IS OKAY, at least on the surface. But just below the surface lies a lot of turbulence. Every now and then one keeps getting sucked in by it. Sometimes one willingly dives in, in the hope that perhaps just facing the turbulence would make it go away. But one only gets tossed from one end to the other with no success. The key lies at the source of the turbulence. But merely identifying the source cannot in itself be a solution. Besides, diving in seems to stir things even more. But then living on the surface too doesn't really feel right; it is only a denial of the situation. I **GUESS** I have no choice but to simply accept the situation and live. Yes, there is turbulence. Yes, have to dive, maybe will myself some silence in the calm of the deep waters of the sea.

43

Still searching for that silver lining. Felt a few more bumps today. **GUESS**, the good days are still not here. Have to hang in there. The worse things get, the deeper I go, the deeper I go, the closer I get to myself, the closer I get to myself, the closer I get to God, the closer I get to God, the further I get away from pain.

44

Another low start to yet another day. But there is peace in writing, to be alone with one's own thoughts, no matter how sad or depressing. There is peace and Quiet strength. Intoxicating peace. Far and away from happiness and misery. Just a beautiful lull. An escape from escape. Still haunted by could-s, would-s and should-s, shattered by 'is' and perplexed by 'now what's'. Have to face the fears and let them go. To move on. Simply move on. Have to say goodbye.

45

Living for tomorrow because of yesterday doesn't feel that great any more. For what will happen tomorrow will happen and what happened yesterday has already happened. None of them have anything to do with today but for the disappointment and the hope. Easier said than done. THE SENSE OF LOSS IS STILL QUITE SEVERE, BUT HAVE TO LIVE THROUGH IT AND STOP USING THE FUTURE AS A CRUTCH. HAVE TO LIVE THROUGH IT.

What Did You Say?

I was in third grade, when suddenly I heard my name being called out in the class. It was my class teacher and with her was the vice-principal of the school. Apparently, the vice-principal had missed the morning assembly and was enquiring about the announcements made. For some reason the teacher chose me to share with the vice-principal what was said and that too in front of the whole class. I walked to the front of the class slowly and stuttered out a couple of incoherent sentences. The teacher, clearly unhappy with my response, said sternly, 'What's the matter with you? Were you sleeping in the assembly?' I uttered a few words and, among ripples of laughter from other students, was dismissed to my seat. My face red with embarrassment, I sat down quietly.

How would I explain to my teacher that she was partially right? I wasn't paying attention during the announcements, but more importantly I was trembling with nervousness at having to say anything in front of the entire class and the vice-principal and that too in English. Not that my English was bad, but I simply lacked the confidence and practice because I came from a simple middle-class family and we usually spoke in Hindi at home.

But that day haunted me for quite a while. I was ashamed and almost felt inferior. Something had to be done! Luckily, the opportunity was just around the corner. Our school was very active in theatre and music and every year we used to have an interhouse one-act play competition which went on for 2-3 days in front of a fairly large audience. It was quite a prestigious event. Although I had been a part of the school theatre workshop, I hadn't really performed in front of such a large audience. This time I decided to audition for a play and promised myself, no matter what happened I would only participate in English plays (the competition was held for both English and Hindi plays). I had to get over my shortcomings.

That attitude has not changed over the years. My focus has always been on my shortcomings and not so much on my strengths, which is a blessing and a curse. Blessing because I've come a long way from where I was, curse because no matter how many links I fix, there is always a 'weaker' link in the chain. A sure-shot path to misery and struggle for your entire life.

Anyway, I auditioned and managed to get a part in the play, which was largely directed by our seniors. All was going well. I was working extra hard on my diction and dialogue delivery. As I was getting comfortable it finally happened!

I got stuck at a rather innocuous line. I clearly remember I was supposed to walk downstage, look around and say, 'Oh, it's so beautiful over here.' I said the line and the entire cast burst out laughing. I wasn't quite sure what they were laughing at, so I looked around and politely joined in. One of the actors corrected me, 'It's not "here", it's "here".' I thought they were pulling my leg, so I smiled and repeated my line and the laughter got even louder. Now I was getting a little nervous because I couldn't understand what the issue was. So I asked the director. It turned out I couldn't pronounce the word 'here'. Every time I tried to say 'here' it would come out 'hair'. I said it five, ten, fifteen times and it always came out 'hair'.

I somehow survived the day, but when I reached home, I could still hear the laughter ringing in my ear. That night I cried. I had tried so hard but just couldn't get a simple word right. But I didn't give up, I have too much pride for that. I practised over and over again, with marbles in my mouth to exercise my tongue, until I got it right. Needless to say, in the coming years, I won several acting awards in school and as I had promised myself, I only acted in English plays. That holds true even today, although now doing English plays is my comfort zone.

They've been many a battle like these that I've had to win, insignificant on the surface, but paramount within. Even today when someone mocks a person because of their accent or mispronunciation, it upsets me. Maybe I'm being oversensitive, but I'm not alone, especially since today language has also become a barometer of self-worth.

46

7 May

LOST again, LOST in the anguish of a dream that didn't come true. Lost in the loss of innocence. If this is growing up, I don't want to grow up. Yes, I miss my innocence, my dream, my walk into the sunset, MY OWN LITTLE HOME and MY OWN LITTLE FAMILY in MY OWN LITTLE HOUSE.

Maybe I need to dream another dream.

47

Too soon to CELEBRATE, have to hold on to the pain. It's GOOD and it's SAFE. It's peaceful and keeps you true to yourself. There will be a time to CELEBRATE, to make JOY, when all this will seem empty and meaningless. But now is not it. No, the mourning period is far from over. Now is not the end of pain. Have to hold on to it and enjoy it. For it is taking me closer to myself. There will be time to rise again and take action but now is not it. Now is the time between the funeral and the resurrection. But rise I will, with all of God's glory and grace, for I have been blessed with His mercy. I thank GOD and all those who were by my side in this journey. But it is too soon even for the 'thank you-s' for it is not over. And I'm not SCARED of PAIN any more, for PAIN only hurts and hurt always passes. Enough said.

I am. No joy. No sorrow. No yesterday, no tomorrows. Only now and only me. Living in the presence of GOD'S mercy.

Alone!

48

15 May

Alone and abandoned. Just watching God's games. NOTHING TO DO, NOWHERE TO GO, just a spectator. Not even waiting for that silver lining or that bright tomorrow any more. Just watching **GOD'S** plans, have to have faith in Him and His ways. He's in the driver's seat, let's see where all He takes me. Feel blessed in this misery, for I'm witnessing **GOD** at work and am part of it. Just hope this is not despair speaking and that there is no **GOD. Nah!** He is there for I feel **HIS** warmth. This prison is my home and in it I live.

> I love my home and
> nobody's going to
> take it away from me.

49

The revelation of GOD'S plans is so exhilarating. Feel blessed to have this opportunity. Yes, I'm **GROWING BUT THERE IS STILL SUCH A LONG WAY** to go. Only wish I could feel OTHERS' PAIN like I feel my own instead of just UNDERSTANDING it. I thank God for my misery.

50

Am I deceiving myself? Am I still waiting?
Waiting for a future that just doesn't exist and
that I so very desperately want. Am still clinging
on to the past, which is never coming back. Is
my faith in GOD just a CONVENIENCE, the ultimate
hope against all odds? Am I running away from
reality? Or am I getting better? For better or
worse I am sincerely trying not to depend on
people. Never want to go through this pain again.

Where Do You Go?

WHERE DO YOU GO

When the rain is hard and home still far

When the wounds are still fresh

And there's already a scar

When silence is too soft

And a whisper too loud

When inside there's loneliness

And outside too large a crowd

WHERE DO YOU GO?

WHERE DO YOU GO

When the high is too high and the low too low

When your heart is all weary

And your mind says I told you so.

When the past you can't forget

And the future you just don't know

When what you have you don't want

And what you don't, you want it so

WHERE DO YOU GO?

WHERE DO YOU GO
When Heaven in not too far
And Hell is waiting somewhere near
When everyone around you screams courage
And all you hear is fear.

WHERE DO YOU GO?

51

I know these days will pass. I know I will be successful. I know things will work out. God is only testing me. I know I will be happy.

NOWHERE TO GO, NOTHING TO SAY

Living in hell and that's where I'll stay
Scared to be happy for it's only followed by pain
Just traces of sunshine in a sky full of rain.

52

LOST BETWEEN WHAT I OUGHT TO FEEL AND WHAT I DO.

It's really funny, when deep down one knows that sooner or later everything will be fine, yet one can't help but worry. One knows that nothing is really in one's hands and that things will take their own course, yet one can't help but struggle. **GUESS**, all roads lead to **GOD**. Anyway, staying away from everyone is doing me good.
I am feeling stronger.

53

31 May

Broken! No respite!

Tired of praying, don't know what to do any more. I **GUESS** I have to let go. Can't show someone what they don't want to see. **HAVE TO TAKE THE BLOWS STANDING. BUT HOW LONG?** I pray to God. Please, God, no more, I've had enough. Mercy! You win, I lose. Please, I beg of you.

54

Words, people ... the only peace that there is, is in sorrow. Better to live in pain and with God than without. In sorrow is silence, beautiful silence, alone, far and away from the cacophony of who said what, when and why. Need the silence to function, just to be normal, need it like oxygen. Pure, unadulterated silence and the STILLNESS that comes with it. STILLNESS of being, not acting or reacting to the past, present or the future. Just a silent observer like the rocks and the trees. In this STILLNESS lies the energy to move, to reach out and to pursue. But right now, it's the quest for silence, away from joy and sorrow, away from today and tomorrow. Far and away deep within, where you only experience love and compassion. You want to heal everyone. Take everyone's pain away. Release them from their chains. You pray for their peace and cry for their trials. Hope **GOD'S** light shines on them and they walk in His heavenly glory. I PRAY FOR YOU AND CARRY YOU DEEP IN MY HEART. You were, you are and will always be.

55

Anger, pain, misery ... Never felt so helpless. Everything seems pointless and useless. The future seems like a child's fantasy. Any course of action in the present seems futile. Seems like there is no choice but to take the hits and cry. As far as God is concerned, I **GUESS** I'll just have to wait. There's nothing to understand, nothing to do but just be, and sit and stare and wait for things to take their own course.

56

Not about pain. anger or retribution. It's about peace, about detachment, about silence, about being solitary, about just being Quiet and peaceful and being able to enjoy it. To be detached from the past and future, to be drawn into the lull of today, quietly.

57

Time for self-assessment.
COURAGE, CHARACTER, STRENGTH, PATIENCE.

I FAILED .

God and I

Growing up I rarely went to temples. In fact, I mocked those who did. I would think to myself, even if God does exist, the last place you would find him/her/it and connect with Him would be in a place with so much chaos and hustle-bustle. To me God was always within me, in fact I would chat with him often and shared a fairly healthy relationship. I can safely say that my faith in God has been the one and only constant thing in my life. I'm not a religious man but I'm an ardent believer in the 'almighty'. But does 'God' really exist? No matter what name you choose to call him (her or it) with? The omnipresent, sitting up above, keeping a track of who is doing, thinking what. The answer is, I don't know. I can't say for a fact that He exists, nor can I say for a fact he doesn't! But I choose to believe that yes, there is a God, a kind, benevolent loving God who really doesn't want anything from us and is not affected by our belief or disbelief. Every time I pray, the thing I ask for most often is the ability to tell right from wrong, have the courage to do the right thing. It is my belief in God that helps me sleep peacefully at night, pick myself up when I'm down and have the courage to attempt the impossible. And I must say my belief has often been tested but rarely has it failed me. Does that mean God exists? Or that my powerful belief in God has created the energy to make things work accordingly. The answer is, as before, I don't know! I guess the thing I truly believe in is Karma, in action and thought. You reap what you sow.

As far as temples and other holy places and rituals are concerned, not so long ago I had a change of heart. We (my wife and I) were celebrating our daughter's third birthday and had organized a kiddies' party. There must have been about fifty-odd kids with their parents or nannies. It was quite a fun evening with music, food, clowns, slides, etc. But I could see from the corner of my eyes that my daughter, instead of enjoying, seemed a little scared. I kept my eyes on her, looking for a hint of what and why she might be feeling that way. Within moments I realized that she was feeling overwhelmed with so many people around – quite a few must have been strangers to her as well. I rushed up to her and took her in my arms. There was a sense of relief in her eyes. For the next couple of minutes, she held me real tight, like she had never done before. After a few moments when she calmed down, she looked at me with tears in her eyes and said, 'I love you, papa.' I didn't know how to react. Holding back my tears I hugged her tight again. I had never experienced this kind of unconditional love before. I saw the world through her eyes and realized what I or my wife meant to her. That night I made a promise to God that henceforth once a week I would go to a temple and pray for her safety. I was inadequate and needed some help, so I went to the only one I trust.

In God I trust,
To Him I surrender
His will shall be done
In this life or the other!

58

The hurt feelings of **CHILDHOOD** are catching up; the feelings of not being good enough or wanted. The recent events have resurrected the demons from the past. The ridicule goes on and on and on. Only faces change but the laughter remains the same. **NOW**, someone else is gloating. And all one can do is work hard and achieve more and more until the laughter can't be heard any more. But how long can one run from one's own shadow thinking one day he'll be able to get rid of it. **How long?** And will one ever be good enough? Will this laughter ever die? **Maybe!** Maybe one day the sun will be directly over my head and when **I LOOK STRAIGHT DOWN**, I will see nothing except how tall I stand. Free at last.

59

SILENT AND PEACEFUL, away from people. The only friend is GOD. Enjoying the lull. Sometimes I feel the need for company and regret it within minutes of the indulgence. Very happy being far and away from people, whether they like me or otherwise. Just want to be. Peace lies in isolation. If there is any dependence, it's perhaps BOOKS, SLEEP, EXERCISE, SUCCESS. One day I will get rid of some of them too. Intoxicating peace, complete silence, no quest even for success, just blissful in the company of me, myself and I.

Streets Of Hell

THE NIGHT WAS LONG

The day not yet quite bright

Maybe the sun had lost some of its lustre

Maybe I just got attached to the night

For when in darkness God's light fell

I found in you my own little heaven

Away from these streets of hell.

60

20 June

WHAT SHOULD JOB DO? What does God want?
Where do the answers lie? In the mind, the heart,
or the spirit? The heart reacts. The mind thinks
and then reacts. The spirit just observes. Be with
the moment. **Job must repent but ...** shouldn't
He heal? Unto God I submit.

61

The silence seems peaceful. But is this my
weakness or my **strength**? Am I running away
from fear or am I facing it? Am I getting
stronger or weaker, moving forward or back?
Am I the valiant warrior or a SCARED spectator
watching from the side? Who is brave? He
who accepts himself for what he is and goes
ahead with life or he who has the courage to
confront himself and TRY TO CHANGE HIMSELF? Am
I running away from life by stopping and
FACING THE PAIN? Yes, I have stuck through. I
have removed all my crutches, friends, work, etc.
Maybe I failed. Just live in the 'now'. The only
crutch is God. CAN'T LET GO OF THAT YET.

62

Getting awfully tired. Just when I start looking forward to something to save the day, God takes it away. Sometimes, I get really tired and feel like giving up everything and running away. Unable to understand life. Fell madly in love with a girl, married her only to find out ... Have put all my eggs in one basket and my heart shudders every time the basket shakes. Tired of being tested. Want peace. No more tests, God, no more! I give up and you win. **I GIVE UP, GOD. WHY MUST I BE TESTED ALL THE TIME? PLEASE NO MORE.**

63

28 June

Excruciating pain continues. Nowhere to run, nowhere to go. Just endless misery.

Hush! Happiness is just around the corner. **Where?**

64

30 June

And so he died every minute,
LITTLE BY LITTLE, PIECE BY PIECE. Until there
was nothing left to die – mind, body or soul.
He was as dead as he could be without dying.
His breath, the only proof of his life ... and lots
and lots of **PAIN**. His hands trembled as tears
fell from his eyes. **Was he crying at his death
or the death of the world as he once knew
it?** Was this really death or the final freedom?
Was this the death of a little boy or the birth
of a grown man? Time to wipe your tears
and get along with your painful but real life.
LITTLE BY LITTLE, PIECE BY PIECE.

Searching For God

I WEEP, I CRY AND LIFE GOES ON

Unhaltingly, mercilessly from dusk to dawn

Have I managed to numb my pain?

Do I need to beat it a little more?

Have I milked my sorrows for all they're worth?

Or is there much more in store?

Broken and tired with only life's emptiness staring at me

I search for God

If He's there

It's time for Him to make an entry.

65

3 July

Many rivers to cross, many mountains to climb and many battles to fight. This is just the beginning. **What is it that makes me cling to the past?** Why still that insane desire to possess, to own. And what does one do about it?

Climbing the Mountain

It's time to be brutally honest. Not that I've been dishonest so far, but I need to peel more layers and dig deeper and hopefully reach the bottom, at least for now, until more layers reveal themselves and I have to dig even deeper. I've been a professional actor for almost twenty-five years and have dreamt of being an actor for over forty years. I wanted to be an actor the moment I attended my very first theatre workshop at the age of eight. So pretty much all my life I've consciously or subconsciously thought and prepared myself to be an actor.

According to the veteran actor John Lithgow, there are five stages in an actor's life:

1) Who is John Lithgow?
2) Get me John Lithgow.
3) Get me someone like John Lithgow.
4) Get me a younger version of John Lithgow.
5) Who is John Lithgow?

Now that I find myself between stages 4 and 5, I ask myself the very difficult question, was it worth it? What was it that drew me to acting? And what is that still keeps the passion burning? Or is it time to move on? And if so, to what? I started my professional life working as a financial analyst on Wall Street, and I was miserable. I decided, with enormous difficulty, to change course and pursue my passion. I didn't realize that enjoying acting or being good at it is very different from being an 'actor', a professional actor. I enjoy writing, I'm adequate at it but that does not make me a 'writer'. Knowing at that time what I know now, would I still have pursued acting as a profession, as opposed to doing it as a 'therapy' or a 'hobby' which I happened to excel in. Wouldn't I have been better off with a 'comfortable' corporate job and do theatre on weekends? And even if I chose to be a professional actor, what made me stick through it for so long and not give up? Was it my passion or my stubbornness or my addiction to this crazy profession where you get to live a thousand lives and emotions?

It's like climbing Mount Everest because it's there, and you enjoy climbing and think you can do a better job than most. So step by step you climb the mountain. There are good days and there are bad days but you keep climbing not because you want to but simply because you think you can. You don't want to look back, because you're afraid you'd question your decision. So you keep trudging along one step at a time, towards a peak you can't even see any more. Sometimes you get exhausted and sit down, you can see tiny little houses in the valley with smoke coming out of the chimneys. You imagine what it would be like to be with your family at the dinner place next to the warm fireplace, food, fun and laughter. It is then you realize the sacrifices you've made, for whenever you focus really hard on one aspect of your life, you compromise another aspect. You can achieve anything but not everything, so choose and expend your energy carefully.

So here you are all alone in the freezing darkness of the tallest mountain in the world, too late to turn back and the top nowhere in sight and you ask yourself: was this madness, what you call passion, worth it? It's your stubbornness that keeps pushing you. You're not even sure you will like the view or be able to enjoy it when you reach the 'top'. You spent your entire life trying to prove to yourself and others that you could and now you don't even care what anyone, including yourself, thinks. All you realize is the price you paid. Some might argue that greatness or anything good comes with a price. God doesn't give you anything without extracting his pound of flesh. Greatness according to whom? And for what? Would you, if given the choice, be the greatest artiste in the history of mankind and die a miserable, lonely death fighting your inner demons and addictions. As much we admire the greats like Michael Jackson, Elvis Presley, etc., not one, if push comes to shove, would trade their 'ordinary' life for theirs. So as Bruce Springsteen sang, 'When you ask for a wish, son, you better think first, for with every wish, there comes a curse.'

6 July

BEING ALONE IS BEAUTIFUL AND PEACEFUL, BUT IT ALSO FEELS NICE TO BE
DESIRED, LOVED, appreciated and recognized. But that
leaves you at the mercy of others and your own
urges. The key lies in silence. Fighting human
weaknesses. Beautiful, blissful silence. **The
quest is for completeness, and silence is the
path. The rest?** They are all details and will
follow.

67

Ghosts of the past keep coming back. What?
Where? And the biggest of them all, now what?
Where do I go from here? I sit alone, lost,
questioning my life. But there aren't any questions
... just have to do what I believe in. Happy, sad,
lazy, idealistic, philosophic, dependent, SCARED,
single-minded, irresponsible, whatever it is, it's
me. I am the way I am; things are the way they
are and that's the way they should be. For better
or for worse, this is me and this is my path. My
inner voice will guide me. I HAVE FAITH IN IT AND I WILL
WAIT QUIETLY AND PATIENTLY for its guidance. The time to
act will come. Yes, I confess I am SCARED. I can
only put everything in God's hands. He has never
let me down. Even in my worst failures, he has
shown me success, in my sorrow, happiness. Show
me your miracle, God, give me the life I seek.

HAST THOU COURAGE TO TRAVEL ALONE YOUR INVISIBLE PATH?

Then carry this lamp in thy hand and walk with steadfast gaze.

Look not back, the past will melt in the dark,

FOLLOW, FOLLOW, FOLLOW ON BY ITS GLOW.

SWAMI PARAMANANDA

68

13 July

Feeling very restless, maybe in anticipation of things to come. Wound up quite tight, unable to settle down. Always seem to be on my toes, at least mentally. The mind has lost its calm and tranquility. Desperately trying to calm down and relax. Have to keep writing to maintain my sanity. This sudden attention and adulation are getting to be quite taxing. Need to calm down, need to relax. Have to have faith in GOD and the course of nature. Everything is happening for the best. GOD will give me the strength to endure. This attention is all bullshit; we come to this world to suffer. That is the way of the BUDDHA. Have to see through these illusions. **Have to stop buying into it before I start judging myself by it.**

69

17 July

EVERYTHING IS CAVING IN. Want to just break down and empty myself out. Things have been building up for a while. **Want to cry**, scream and let it all out but just not able to do so. Need help, please, please somebody somewhere help me. Is this my life I'm living, one depression after another? Am I jinxed to a life of endless battles? Will there ever be smooth sailing? **Tired, very tired. Yet another mirage.**

Nowhere To Run

NOWHERE TO RUN, NOWHERE TO HIDE,

Nowhere to rest and just ride the tide,

Broken and shattered, don't know what to do

Need help, a little something to get me through

Tears are drying but no help coming,

Hope is dying and only more despair coming.

They say, do what is right, that is all there is to do,

But how does one do when one does not know

What it is that one has to do.

70

20 July

Restless. TIME TO TAKE STOCK. Things are falling into place. Can feel it. Getting ready for a change. Good times are just around the corner. Can feel the momentum building up. JUST AROUND THE CORNER COMES THE LIGHT OF DAY.

71

24 July

Gloomy, grey, yet another lull.

Before or after the storm, who knows? No traces left of the last storms or hints of the ones to come. Just a lull after a lull and after yet another lull. A somewhat eerie stillness. Hints of abandonment. THAT'S OKAY. EVEN GOD NEEDS A BREAK. Hope he comes back soon. No pain, no joy, not even any peace, just an anxiety-ridden lull.

72

Thoughts of the betrayal keep coming back.
Don't want to be 'UNDERSTANDING' any more.
Don't want to give the benefit of DOUBT.

73

NUMB!
DEVOID OF FEELINGS.
Only traces of hurt, anger and rejection. No
God, no nothing.

74

THERE HE SAT ALL ALONE WITH ALL HIS **demons** AND **fears**. ALONE WITH AN UNPLEASANT PAST, an uncertain future and a non-existent present. There is no refuge. The past, the present and the future, each bleaker than the other. HE WAS PERHAPS WAITING FOR AN **angel** to comfort him and tell him that everything was going to be just fine but he probably wouldn't even let an angel take care of him. Everything was bullshit. The only truth was the loss and the pain.

The loss of what was and couldn't and the pain of what could have and did not.

Bhindi with Paratha

Igrew up in a fairly conservative yet 'non-religious' Hindu family. Apart from Diwali, Dussehra and maybe Janamashthami, we didn't really celebrate too many festivals or go to temples often. Mom would do a small puja twice a day, but for Dad, his religion was work hard, being a good human being and helping whoever he could. The word he hated most was 'can't'. He would tell us that the word 'impossible' did not exist in his dictionary. He hailed from a small village in Himachal. He had minimal education and had been fending for himself since he was a teenager. He made enough money to educate his children abroad. Being respectful was very high on his list, specially to women. No one in the family used tobacco or consumed alcohol. For some strange reason we never had the urge either. Only in my late twenties did I become a social drinker, but till date I don't really enjoy or look forward to it. My two elder brothers, both above fifty, don't smoke or drink. I guess the fruits don't fall too far from the tree. Till the day Dad passed away, the thing he was most proud of was his children being well behaved and well educated.

Helping people, however he could, even if it meant us cutting corners was very important to him. Whenever my mother confronted him, he'd say, what's money but dirt of your hands, I'll work harder and make more. Saying no to anyone was impossible for him. He'd go out of his way to take favours for those in need. Helping others was part of his religion and he usually kept it a secret from us, in case anyone, especially Mom, objected. Mom would tell him, you don't have to be so large-hearted that people cheat you. They would have heated arguments, but he was very much his own man and extremely stubborn. Once his mind was made up nothing could change it (Mom says I've inherited this trait from him and like him money doesn't hold too much value for me).

Once when I was a kid, like we did every summer break, we were going to Simla. We always went by train as there were no direct flights from Delhi to Simla. We travelled non-AC. I don't know if it was to save money or whether AC class didn't exist at the time. It used to be a lot of fun, sitting by the window, watching the countryside with isolated huts go by. I used to wonder what life in those villages would be like. I'm sure they didn't have television or newspapers. How did they keep track of time or what day it was or whether that was important to them at all? I almost envied them. And then at night the train would stop at this isolated, small station with no more the two or three people, the guard with the red-green flag, the station master in his uniform and a boy selling hot tea and samosa. My brother and I would step out for a bit to stretch our legs and feel the change of temperature. It would be a bit nippy. Simla must be close, we'd deduce.

Another part of travelling by train was carrying those cumbersome roll-up mattresses. This was for the one who slept on the floor, as sleeper cabins usually had six berths. During the day the middle two berths were folded to make more space for other people. You pretty much got to know half the bogey. For some strange reason there would always be at least one young newly-wed couple going for the honeymoon. The coy looks they exchanged, with this scrawny guy trying to act like a man and trying to take care of his almost child bride. The bride still had her mehendi and the choora she must have worn in the shaadi. It was adorable. Then there would always be this middle-aged overweight, balding, overfriendly uncle with a combover. He was the one who kept everyone in splits, telling anecdotes and insisting on everyone tasting his mother's bhindi with paratha. Before you knew it, there was a buffet, everyone opening their respective tiffins and sharing with everyone. Those were such simpler days. I sometimes wonder what happened to that world? Did people change or did I? Do people still greet each other with the same warmth? Or have we all evolved into self-absorbed creatures who don't know how to interact with other people without the aid of technology? Even in a four-by-four-foot lift, we stare at our phones or look at the elevator display instead of greeting each other with a smile and venture into a hello.

75

4 August

WOW!, WHAT A DAY! Swung from one extreme to the other like a **yo-yo**. First, beat myself up then pulled myself up, and then beat myself yet again and now trying to pull myself up again. Sometimes I defy all definitions of logic or sanity. **GOD**, have mercy!

76

Yet another a day without hope, no silver
lining, not even a lost ray of the sun. Only
dark morbid skies. The grey is getting more and
more real and not easily dispelled by hope of
a brighter tomorrow. FAR TOO MANY BRIGHT tomorrows
have lost their lustre on their way to today
and yesterday. However, one still looks forward
to yet another tomorrow to make today more
bearable. But this game is getting ridiculous,
for far too many todays have come and gone.
Perhaps in just giving yourself up and lying
still lies the key. But in it there's also hope and
hence the anticipation and the struggle. Only in
hopelessness seems hope. Have to lose all hope. It
will probably happen by itself anyway; there have
been too many mirages, too many stray logs,
too many little islands on the horizon.

77

ANOTHER MISERABLE MORNING.
Did not really want to get up but
did so nevertheless, hoping maybe,
just maybe today ... but no,
GOD is missing again.
Hate being alone. Miss my own little family.

Together Again

SAW THE HEAVEN AGAIN, SAW ITS GLORY AGAIN,
Saw a different ending to the same old story again.
Heard the birds sing, heard the bells ring
Saw the dead flowers blossom in the middle of the spring again
Saw God again, saw Him smile again
Saw His mercy in the times of despair again
Saw me again, saw you again
Saw each other love one another again.

78

The mind keeps going in circles, rearranging facts. Desperately trying to find a perspective from which the reality is more acceptable. But these are all mind games. The truth and the reality comprise how one actually feels. 'Whys' and 'why nots' are just games played by the mind to come to **TERMS** with reality. The reality is that I am lonely, I am disappointed with my work and I am unable to come to terms with my broken marriage. And while one keeps feeling these emotions, the **MIND** keeps on ticking, pushing one to change the existing reality. Until a new reality is created and a new set of emotions replace the existing ones, the mind plays whatever games, giving different colours to memories to make the present more **livable**.

79

Success, money, fame ... in the end the only thing that comes to your rescue is **GOD** and your faith in Him. Yes, there is more to life. But sometimes we get stuck in endless loops and are unable to see beyond ourselves. We run, driven by one fear or another, in our endless attempt to fill our incompleteness. The chase is futile but essential because it eventually leads you to yourself through **GOD**. You do things because you want to and not because you are **SCARED** or you need to, and you eventually discover that things always work out, one way or the other. It has been a long journey but now I'm heading home.

24 August

Anger, rage, wrath. Save me ... Heal my pain, take away my anger and stop my wrath. 'FOR WRATH KILLS A SIMPLE MAN AND ENVY SLAYS A FOOLISH ONE' (Job 5:2).

81

28 August

Same old emptiness takes over. But that's okay. AFTER ALL, THESE ARE TESTING TIMES. Just have to hang in there. Just have to lie low while the tide is still against me. It's not going to be *easy*...

82

1 September

PLEASANT MORNING, half-baked thoughts, scattered mind, no clarity, only a jumble of thoughts and **EMOTIONS.** Perhaps this is what a hangover is all about. Late night, inane conversations, pointless, meaningless...

83

6 September

Nothingness. No distractions will do. Have to face up to my own fears, sorrows and incompleteness. There's peace within but have to struggle through barriers of pain to reach there. It's exhausting but there really is no other way. Have to go through the PAIN, ANGER and FRUSTRATION. But it is getting better and very soon all this will be gone. Not because there will be better days but because there will be total ACCEPTANCE. Whether I have my day or not remains to be seen. Until then there is a new thing to be learnt every day. And slowly and surely am becoming a better man.

10 September

The PAIN goes on but so does my **determination**. In the name of GOD, I hold on, taking each blow on my chin. The hits keep coming but I stand my ground, for the night shall pass and the sun will rise, and I'll still be standing there when the final bell rings.

Land of the Rising Sun

IN THE LAND OF THE RISING SUN

I walk with the night behind me

And the morning light in front

It has been a long hard

night but I walked through it all

Unflinchingly, incessantly

Through each swamp, each fall

With my feet firmly on the ground

And my eyes fixed to the sky

I fought each fear,

Never once asking why

For I knew behind these fears lay the real key

Where I would meet the

Real, fearless, complete me.

No doubt, no fear

Not even a trace of uncertainty

Just me, my God and in me

His strength of eternity

Yes, walk in the land of the rising sun

For I know, all it takes to end this long dark night
Is just one little
Ray of the shining sun.

85

My problems, my fears, my pain are all mine.
No one else is responsible for them. They are
mine and I will not share them with anyone.
It's between GOD and me and no one has the
right to intervene. Just Him and me. The rest,
everyone and everything, is inconsequential. It's
His plan against my will. It does seem a little
unfair because any which way I win. If I win, I
win, and If He wins, still I win. Although I still
hope I win because one likes to hold on to the
known. But my experience tells me that if He
wins, I win much bigger because I am limited
by my narrow vision. Just the realization is so
exhilarating. It's as if your birthday is coming
and GOD is in charge of the party. What more can
one ask for? Patience, there is still time to open
the gifts. Patience.

86

20 September

Another day of living with rejection, not being good enough. I know it's not true but that doesn't matter as long as that's the way I feel. There is not a morning that I don't get up with a sense of being less than. It's like standing in line with all you've got and then someone comes along and tells you, 'SORRY, that's just not good **enough.**' But I **GUESS** in some ways I've never been good **enough, constantly** trying to prove it to the world – so maybe one day I'll truly start believing it myself. This obviously has nothing to do with reality but then 'REALITY' doesn't matter, for everything is what you perceive it to be. NEED TO FIX THE DISTORTION.

My Second 'This Is It' Moment

A rather painful and heartbreaking memory. I was part of a TV show, probably the most popular show on all channels at the time, which is saying a lot. My character was supposed to be there for a handful of episodes. At the time I was quite disillusioned with films and my career, so very hesitatingly I accepted the cameo. As luck would have it, my character became so popular that the cameo went on for over a year and by the end I became one of the most popular faces on TV. Finally, the gods had smiled at me. There was a nationwide poll for the most popular actor on that TV channel, and I won by a landslide. That evening I went to the beach near my house and wept in the dark. God does work in mysterious ways, because just a year back I was at the same beach crying not knowing what the future held for me. It was a vindication. Finally, everyone had realized what I always knew. I was *good*! I wasn't just another delusional actor with fantasies of grandiosity. My dream to be a successful actor was based on my belief in my ability and my refusal to give up.

There was an award function scheduled the following week, acknowledging the most popular actors, directors, producers, shows, etc. It was a foregone conclusion that my female co-star and I were winning in the popular actor category. There we were in the wings, teasing each other like kids and waiting for our names to be announced. Her name was announced and off she went with a knowing see-you-soon smile. She happily received her award to an ovation and a speech of gratitude. Now it was my turn, I took a deep breath, trying to calm down my racing heart. 'And the award for most popular actor male goes to...' I started walking towards the stage, and suddenly lightning struck! Someone else's name was announced! I was dumbfounded. What had just happened? Surely there was a mistake. I looked around helplessly. I was told that I had won, my name was on the teleprompter the host was reading off, all day everyone had been congratulating me but somehow I was watching someone else receive 'my award'.

Heartbroken and seething with anger I stormed out of the auditorium. I hadn't wanted to come for this function in the first place (as something similar had happened before), but they had assured me that this time it wouldn't, that I had indeed won by a huge margin. But alas, my need for validation had got the better of me. Some feeble excuses were given and even a 'consolation award' was announced. But the moment had passed and by that time I was already in my car, distraught and disillusioned. I was so close and yet so far. Sometimes, I feel God is a mean prankster and likes to mess with our hopes and expectations or maybe I was just born to be the second best or the third best or … never the winner. Or maybe it's the curse, the more you want something the further it goes away from you. Detachment is the key – a lesson I would learn for my next 'this is it' moment!

25 September

How does one weep for the past as it continues
to haunt me. Everything, anything seems to
remind me of it.
**Why did I...? Why couldn't I...? Why
couldn't I let go of something that was once
my life?** Constantly bouncing between guilt,
pain, rejection and a lot of anger. But these are
all my emotions and hence my responsibility.
Being solitary seems to be the only thing
that gives me peace. **To be alone with my
thoughts ... is it dreaming, is it depression,
meditation, or simply, wallowing in my
sorrow?** Perhaps this is all part of the healing
process. Face the present, accept the past ... And
the future? **GUESS** I will have to take it as it
comes. Until then it is one long nightmare.

27 September

ALONE WITH MY THOUGHTS. Maybe not, for I do have my fears, my hopes, my pain. No, not alone at all, but yes, very, very lonely. Despair is seeping in. Just two choices ...search for a silver lining or just drift. The former is too TAXING and, after all, how long? The latter comes with its own set of fears. Just have to BREAK DOWN and CRY and fall asleep and then drift some more.

30 September

It is always tough going to sleep with so many
faces in your mind and waking up all alone.
All night long, images flood your mind. Warm,
happy moments, when everything seemed so
right and so perfect. A **BLINK** of the eye and they
are all gone. Those smiling faces, those tender
moments, that heart-filled **LAUGHTER**, replaced
by stark, hollow **EMPTINESS**. Your mind wants to
sleep some more so it can relive those moments
just one more time, but no, even as the laughter
still echoes in your mind, it's all gone. Hate you,
GOD, hate you.

2 October

Have to write, for there is no peace without it. Unable to calm my mind or be in touch with myself without writing. Still clinging on to the past. I wish I could go back to the past and relive those beautiful moments. Do not want to replace them with anyone or anything. I will deal with the situation the only way I know, silently and alone. Yes, there is comfort in this misery. Somehow not too concerned about the future. There will be hardships and heartaches but what will be, will be and eventually it will be good. Not too concerned about success either. I know it can't avoid me for long. Sooner or later it has to find its way to me. I know I am on the right path. Until then, I will enjoy my trials and tribulations.

91

7 October

SUCCESS, AWARDS, RECOGNITION, etc., all
seem so much **bullshit**. Really not worth losing
your sleep over. In the end it really doesn't
matter. The only effort worth putting in is in
being in touch with yourself. The rest are just
trivialities.

92

WRITING, a path to yourself. Tiring but rewarding. It gets tough to cut through the layers to reach the core. One would rather just drift. But drifting seems to be even more exhausting because of the chaos of thoughts running through one's mind. No energy to cut through the haze. Will just coast along for a while.

93

ANOTHER CRUCIAL DAY APPROACHING. Is it
going to be another mirage, another floating log
that's **GOING** to just drift by or is there going to
be finally some rain after all the **lightning?**
But I **GUESS** I can take some more. Have got
attached to the prison. Even the thought of
leaving it **SCARES** me. Perhaps I am afraid of
being disappointed. Perhaps I am disappointed
that no one let me out. I don't want your
freedom, love or success, I am happy alone with
my sorrow. Don't need no help or sympathy or
any friends, family or GOD. Tired of GOD'S games.
Maybe I'll be happy when I am finally successful
but as of now, I don't want it. **GUESS** I am too
SCARED to want anything. How long can one live
the todays on the hope of a better **tomorrow?**
Really don't need anyone to share my joys
and sorrows, to wipe my tears and put me to

sleep. No, thank you, I can do it myself. It's all bullshit, nothing really matters. Anything is okay as long as it gets you through the day without screwing up your tomorrow. **You'll be all right, Sammy, don't worry.**

94

15 October

Pain of rejection, fear of loss. Love, still the
ultimate escape. The need to be loved, to be
wanted, to be needed, to run back into the
security of someone's arms. SCARED, waiting
outside. **What happened? Where has
everyone gone? Will they come back? Will I
be left alone?** GOD, it's getting dark. Please send
them back. I'm SCARED and there are strangers
all around me. Please GOD, please send them
back. He was four years old.

95

18 October

How do you feel, Samir Soni? Running on empty, very lonely and very tired. Need someone to love. My escape from reality, escape from the relentless pain. But SCARED of letting people get too close to me, scared that they might see through my facade of perfection. UNABLE TO FUNCTION.

96

22 October

SCARED? DEPRESSED? Not quite sure which way life is heading or what the future holds. Don't even know if what I am doing, sitting and waiting, is right. Have **lost** my **smile**.

97

24 October

UNABLE TO GET WHAT I WANT. Don't want what I get. And where does that leave me? Depressed, alone and frustrated. Tried COMPROMISING but that didn't get me too far.

98

27 October

THERE HE SAT alone **crying**, day after day, night after night, till he couldn't cry no more. And then he cried some more. He wanted to cry until every trace of pain was washed away, for he knew that tears were his only atonement and pain his companion. He had lost everything he ever had and there was nothing else left to fear except pain. **And how long and how much could the world hurt him?** Seething with anger and indignation he dared the world to give him more pain. And with burning determination in his eyes, he took every bit of IT UNFLINCHINGLY. In his heart he knew that they would eventually get tired while he would emerge stronger because, with each blow, he would become aware of yet another chink in his **armour**. Soon there would be no chinks left to **hurt**. All they were doing were unmasking themselves and pushing him to his eternal source of strength. The more they pushed, the stronger he got, and now he was running wildly at them, chest out, shoulders upright, clothes drenched with blood, screaming, 'More, more, give me more.' Suddenly there was a shocked silence and everyone started to back away. For he had taken their worst and they had nothing else to hit him with. One by one they backed into their **own little worlds**, stunned into silence by what had happened. He stopped and looked towards the sky. He knew his test was finally over. He had nothing left to prove to anybody. He stood there alone in the middle of the town, his SHOULDERS SLOUCHED and his head down with fatigue, tired from the thousands and thousands of years of battle. As he wiped his tears, he looked around for one last time before walking away, vowing never to return to the town, ever again.

99

1 November

NO RESPITE. Unable to understand why I
still have hope. Absolutely no reason to feel
optimistic under the circumstances. No idea what
God has in store, don't know if I want to know
either. Just wonder how long this will go on, how
long I can live like this. Is this really my life
that **I'm living?** Too tired to even try to **SUCCEED.**
Fed up of being the good loser. Just want things
to fall in place, once and for all.

Crest and Trough

I remember reading a short story when I was about ten years old, an anecdote narrated by an actor from his childhood. Every Sunday afternoon this young boy (the actor) and his father would go for a swim in the sea. The boy, like his father, was a pretty good swimmer and with his father by his side, he always wanted to go further and further into the sea. The father kept a sharp eye on the son and how far deep they were going.

One day, the boy, in his enthusiasm, swam a little further than they normally did. The current started to get rough, but the boy, knowing his father was right behind him, gleefully swam on. But soon the boy heard his father's stern voice, 'That's it, no more, the tide is getting stronger.' The boy hesitated for bit but hearing the urgency in his father's voice, turned around and started to swim back towards the beach. However, the sea got rougher and started to drag them further into the sea. The high tide had come sooner than they had anticipated. Even the sky had become overcast and looked like it was going to rain.

The boy started to panic. The harder he tried to swim towards the shore the further the tide seemed to drag him back. But the boy did not give up. With his heart pounding and lungs exploding, he swam on. Suddenly, he felt his father's hand over his arm. He heard him say, 'Relax, don't struggle.' The boy looked at his father. Much to his surprise, his father was barely moving his arms or legs or even breathing heavily. 'Don't waste your energy,' the father said, 'the tides move back and fro. When it moves against you, be still and conserve your energy, don't try to out-swim the tide. The moment the tide moves towards the shore, swim with all you have.' The boy calmed down and started paying attention to the movement of the tides. Slowly but surely, they started inching towards the shore.

I don't know if it's a true story or not but it taught me the most valuable lesson of my life. Time! As you go through life, there are good times and there are bad times and the lull between them. When the times are good, no matter what you do, the results are always favourable. Even if you try you can't put a wrong foot forward. Make the most of it because as sure you're of day and night, the 'bad' times are waiting just round the corner. No matter what you do, how hard you work, things will go against you. You can fight against these times, cry yourself hoarse 'Why me', but these times you have to endure. This is the time to be still and try to understand what lesson life is trying to teach you. And finally, when there is a lull in your life, brace yourself, for another cycle of crest and trough is on its way.

100

No, no, can't ... don't want to ... hate it ... why should I?
DON'T NEED TO, DON'T BELIEVE IN IT ... CAN'T DO ANYTHING just for the sake of doing something. Please don't make me do it, please God! PLEASE ... OKAY, dammit, when do we start?

101

I bow to GOD and accept his will. I yield my plans, dreams and aspirations to him and thank him for the silence. **Yes, I still hold on** to the past and that's okay with me. Perhaps the time to let go has not come as yet. But in my misery and pain I am happy because it has kept me closer to GOD. Wish things had worked out differently, but who am I to question GOD'S will? **I thank you for everything.**

102

The strings that bind us ... far and yet not far
enough, near and yet not near enough. Can't
break them or strengthen them. Only hold on.
Sometimes I wonder what GOD wants. Every
time I dream of a miracle, I'm woken up by
yet another setback. And just when I am about
to give up, He gives another twist to the story.
One way or the other He keeps my past very
much a part of my present. BUT IT'S OKAY,
for I accept his will and no matter what, I'm
not going to leave his side and will not let him
leave mine.

Patience ... and the rest shall follow.

103

Life is beautiful again. But for a few scattered thoughts in the periphery, the mind is completely in the present. The sea is alive but not rough. Even the breeze is gentle and caressing. The birds seem to be playfully chasing each other. There is **peace**, there is **silence**, and there is nature's welcoming embrace for the weary traveller. After a long, long time I can breathe again, even if only for a few moments. The journey has been long, **gruelling** and testing, but somehow, falling, stumbling, I've hung in there and I'm proud of myself. I know it's not over yet, but I sense the gates of heaven nearby. I may not be able to see them but I feel them, and I know I am on the right path. It will be rough: there will be THUNDER, there will be LIGHTNING, there will be GHOSTS of the past, TEMPTATIONS of a false tomorrow, but I will just keep on WALKING, head down, GAZE AHEAD, STEP BY STEP.

Mind Games

IN MY HEAD

Sorting, searching

Going down the rabbit hole

Getting to the bottom

Can feel a sense of calm

Is this escapism or just not being reactive?

WHO CARES,

Eyes shut,

Heartbeat slowing down

Slow long breaths

I want to stay here forever

Better than any drug

Or anything else the world has to offer

I FEEL LOVE

Or what I think it feels like

There is no sense of self.

104

23 November

NOT WHAT I WANTED FROM LIFE, not what I thought life would be. Never thought I would be so alone, but I will not reach for the easier way. Only **wish** ... a little too late I **GUESS**.

105

26 November

Quiet morning. For the nth time went to sleep with a million warm memories on my mind and woke up to a cold empty house. I **GUESS** it really doesn't matter, just have to wait on God.

106

And Job cried for mercy. **Why did he have to be the special one? Why couldn't he be just like the rest? Why was he to be tested again and again and again?** WAS THIS THE PRICE FOR HIS EVENTUAL IMMORTALITY? Or was it the price for his past karma? Whatever it was, day by day began his submission to GOD. It was as if he had to be completely destroyed before he was resurrected piece by piece, bone by bone. He witnessed his destruction. TIME AND AGAIN, he would try to resist his metamorphosis but in vain, for GOD had already made up His mind. The resistance, habitual, the destruction, inevitable, and pain, the only path. How long will Job suffer his chastening and thank GOD for it? I give up, do as you please. I give up.

107

CAUGHT in the rut of thoughts, feelings and emotions, ANGER, PAIN, FEAR, frustration and rejection. People, they either need you, or want you to need them, or both. ONE WORSE THAN THE OTHER.

The Little Boy

I'm a liar

I'm a cheat

I'm nothing like

WHAT YOU MEET

I'm whatever you're not

If you're yin

I'm yang

Yes, I'm good at this

And I'm good at that

BUT THAT'S NOT

The real me

I have a void

I'm trying to fill

I've spent my entire life

And I've come up with nil

A FEW KIND WORDS

Acceptance and respect

So the little boy can finally rest.

And doesn't need me to protect.

108

SO THE ADDICT STILL SEEKS HIS DRUG. One-and-a-half years of rehabilitation and still not cured. But luckily God is there to ensure strict discipline, for whenever one even thinks about taking an easier path, He puts the 'no entry' sign in front. But it gets so lonely sometimes, to be home alone on cold rainy nights. The desire to have somebody beside you, to whisper sweet nothings, to just sit together and watch it rain. In each other's arms. I **GUESS** not yet. It's amazing how, in moments like these, God lets his presence felt. It's as if He is guiding me to be strong, to experience as much loneliness as I possibly can. No crutch for **GOD'S** favourite child. Perhaps **HE'S** preparing me for Heavenly glory. After all the prince has to go through severe tests before he is handed his kingdom. Don't know whether to laugh or cry.

It's tough, it's very painful. This self-denial gets extremely tiring and frustrating but one can hardly imagine what treasures wait. If the tests are going to be so severe, how sweet are the rewards going to be!

Sometimes I worry about being delusional or simply CRAZY, but I know, my GOD is there and He does speak to me. Every time I feel myself drowning, He comes along and picks me right up and just when I'm beginning to get comfortable, He goes and throws me right back into the deep sea. It's as if He wants me to learn to swim the rough seas, or maybe He is like a little child who misses the attention He gets when we are not in trouble. Perhaps He simply wants me to see through the illusions of rough and calm waters, between drowning and surviving, between joy and sorrow. Yes, my GOD doesn't fool me any more because I know His plans. Sometimes I do wonder in amazement, why me? On other desperate times, such as cold, rainy, lonely nights like tonight, I find myself asking the same question, but this time in frustration, 'Why me?' And the answer **both the times** ... well, I **GUESS** I am glad it was me.

109

10 December

Same old friend loneliness again. But
it is silly to expect anything else when one
lives in isolation. **BESIDES,** he who conquers
loneliness conquers all and what better way to
experience loneliness than living in isolation?
For loneliness is the experience of living with
oneself, with one's decisions, fears, regrets,
rejections, pain, etc., – by and large all negative
emotions. Perhaps, negative emotions only
because we never really face them. We tend to
brush all these emotions under a carpet and
try to 'get on with our lives', pretending that
none of the related experiences ever happened.
We deal with the good experiences very well,
because we live and relive them. We share them
with everyone around us and are comfortable
with them. **BUT** negative emotions keep getting
stored in our system because we don't express

them or simply don't know how to. We are SCARED to be alone because the moment we are alone, all these negative emotions come rushing back to us, as we are forced to relive all our negative experiences again. Hence, this constant urge to call someone, watch TV, pick up a book – anything to avoid the discomfort of being alone. But unless we deal with the baggage that we have accumulated since childhood, we will never realize our true potential, professionally or personally. **Once the rug has been swept clean**, you will be shining like a diamond and every dream and desire would just be a minor detail. For you would have realized the ultimate quest. Completeness in isolation is loneliness, through loneliness is completeness and in completeness is the eternal energy to achieve anything.

110

DAY IN AND DAY out the mind relives the past. Everywhere I go, something or the other reminds me of it. Over and over again I experience the same PAIN and ANGUISH. BEFORE I KNOW IT, I'm seething with anger and DISBELIEF. But soon it all passes and all I am left with is a sense of loss and EMPTINESS.

111

18 December

Milking pain for all it is worth. Reliving the past in the hope that eventually it will lose some of its bite. But new incidents crop up every day, adding insult to INJURY. And all one can do is cry some more. A rather extended MOURNING, but have no choice really.

112

It's getting tiring! Just want to run into somebody's arms and forget this world for a while.

113

He no longer knew whether he was getting better or simply more accustomed to the pain. Just when he would start to believe that he was indeed getting **BETTER**, he would feel yet another stab. For a moment there would be a sharp shooting pain, followed by helpless resignation as his body hit the floor. **A helpless mesh of flesh and blood.** He had been knocked down the wrong way so many times that sometimes he wondered if he was going about all this right or was it that he was simply destined for more **PUNISHMENT**. Every once in a while, in the darkness he would scream, **'Enough'**, but it didn't really matter. Morning would come and he would try to rise again and by night he would be back on the floor, limp and lifeless. **God** had him really **confused**. He was getting really tired of **justifying God's actions**. 'Because He loves me. Because He wants me to be **strong**. Because He has other plans for **me** … because, because, **because...**' He was getting really tired of his helpless misery and he just wanted this pain to end. **Unfortunately**, he was gifted with **a lot of patience** and that meant he could take more, much more of it. But he didn't want any more. Whether he could take more or not was no longer the issue. He just wanted his pain to end. With these thoughts in his mind and tears in his eyes, he put the pen down, preparing for yet another night of penance and **prayers for relief.**

114

31 December

ALONE. QUIET in my cocoon. Feel the nip in the air.
Reminds me of Diwali time while growing up
in Delhi. Diwali always announced the arrival
of two events. ONE, THE WINTERS. It was time to pull
out the woolens from the trunks, all neatly
folded among mothballs to keep them safe.
I always looked forward to this old leather
jacket, passed down from two generations of
elder brothers. **But hey, a leather jacket**,
regardless of its age, is a leather jacket.
Especially since none of my friends had one.
Yes. it was cool. A TWELVE-YEAR-OLD WITH A
LEATHER JACKET, a pair of **tight Levi's jeans**
and **Adidas** sneakers that my uncle had sent
from **Dubai**, and long hair way past my eyes.
The jeans were a size big but the local tailor
who specialized in jeans ALTERATIONS did a TERRIFIC
JOB. **Life was style.**

But there was also this UNEASINESS in the air. Was it because the season was changing? Yes, it would get dark sooner; and it would definitely feel **a lot quieter too**. There would be fewer people on the road; even the birds seemed awfully quiet. There was this eeriness, especially in the evenings with the fog setting in, lending a ghost-like quality to everything around you. It almost felt as if something **ominous** was approaching. ONCE NIGHT FELL, things would seem much calmer and cosier, **specially inside** the house. All doors and windows would be shut to keep the cold out, even the lights felt nice and warm. IT WAS ALMOST fun to change into your kurta pajamas with Dad's old V-neck sweaters, and settle down to study. Life was warm and secure.

The second thing that Diwali announced was the coming of exams. Maybe that's why everything felt the way it did. Because it was time to burn the midnight oil after a whole year of goofing around. BUT IT STILL felt nice, the house was warm. Through the shut doors of my room, I could hear Mom in the kitchen, shouting at the servants. My elder brother trying to taste the dinner even before it was cooked and little Tommy barking the arrival of Dad from work. **It was my home and that was my family and life's** only worry was to do well in exams. I always believed that the solution to all life's problems was doing well in school, the key to happiness was coming first. Funnily enough, I somehow find myself still thinking the same – doing well at work will somehow solve all problems. But it never did, never does and probably never **will**.

GUESS I never realized that all my doing well was a means to seek affection, approval. Hence, this constant, desperate urge to make everyone happy and be THE CENTRE OF ATTENTION. But how long can one buy people's affections and one's own self-worth with achievements? How long can one keep on chasing that pot of gold in search of that ever-elusive 'happiness'. Yes, success is losing some of its lustre, and yet the heart can't understand what the mind so clearly sees.

My Final 'This Is It' Moment

It had been an excellent year for me. I had got married, was an integral part of an extremely popular reality show and also part of a very successful daily soap, for which I had won several awards. But my eyes were set on one prestigious award which came at the end of the year. Winning this award would be the cherry on the cake and I had a pretty good shot at winning it. My ever-elusive 'this is it' moment. I was excited and nervous. There I was in the first row, dressed in my finest designer clothes, sitting with my beautiful wife. Will I? Won't I? If I did, what would I say, if I didn't, how much would it suck. Entertainment award functions tend to be a long-drawn-out process, often stretching well over four hours. Four hours can be extremely challenging; applauding, smiling for the camera, waving out to people you may or may not know, it's dark and you don't want to be rude, pretending to be interested in what's going on on the stage, while deep down you want to be home in your pyjamas watching something on your iPad. The function, for some reason, was being held in an open field and as it turned out, it was an intolerably hot and humid evening. It was getting rather unbearable in my fitted black suit and I started 'thinking', *bad idea*! *What the hell am I doing here*?

Besides the arduously long proceeding, my fake smile, the sauna we were sitting in, my anxiety had kicked in. I guess one shot of vodka before you leave your house lasts only so long.

I wasn't enjoying the evening. If I won, it wasn't really going to prove anything regarding how good or bad an actor I was, yet I wanted it! Maybe I wanted it because of the bragging rights it would give me or maybe because I could finally deliver 'my Oscar' speech; this time my wife was there, as also people knew who I was (so applause was guaranteed) and I honestly believed I deserved it. This was going to be *the* 'this is it' moment that I had been waiting for. The proceedings went on and I hung in there. As time went by, oddly enough I started feeling more and more confident; maybe it was because of the smiles I was getting from the organizers. By the fourth hour I had started finetuning my speech. The best actor's award is usually given at the very end of the event with a lot of fanfare. I was ready. Mount Everest was just a step away and then it happened. I did indeed win the best actor's award and yes there was applause, albeit a little muffled, but as I started to make my walk to the stage, the lights began to go off. I looked around and people had started to get up from their seats. *What's going on*? I thought to myself. Had there been a terrorist attack? Or was it simple technical malfunction? If so, why *now*?

As it turned out, the ceremony had exceeded the duration for which it was permitted and they had to wind up. As I reached the stage, more than half the people had left, some because their category was done and others to avoid the traffic on their way home. As I received the holy grail, people were passing right in front of me, calling for their drivers. By the time I reached the mic, and began my speech, the sound had been switched off. But since this event was going to be telecast on TV, the camera was still rolling. So I smiled and waved to the empty chairs and mumbled a few words, blew a kiss towards my wife and that was it! Yes, I might be exaggerating a little bit, there might have been a hundred-odd people still there, of the almost thousand. But, yes, I spoke into a soundless mic to an almost non-existent audience. I couldn't help but laugh inside. What are the odds of something like this happening, and this was going to be my crowning glory? The desire for awards and recognition has drastically declined since then. Once in a while I still fantasize about it but always wryly and never without a smile. This is it, indeed! All those years of hearing about doing your karma and not being attached to the outcome, I always had one eye on the goal and only one eye on the path. Older and wiser.

Born To Be Free

I'M GETTING OLD
I'M GETTING OLD

No longer able to do

the things I was told

How long can one say

Just wait and see

When life has passed you by

And you're nowhere near

Where you thought you'd be

But it's not over yet, that's a fact

There is still some time for the final act

So I pick myself up one more time

Assess the situation and draw the line

WHAT IS GONE IS IN THE PAST

Hopefully I did justice to how I was cast

Far off at the end of the tunnel I can see

My sweet Lord smiling at me

Don't lose hope, son

Life has just begun

NIGHT'S ALMOST OVER

Round the corner is the shining sun

I'm sorry for what I put you through

How else would you discover the real you

For you are not what you've been told

Bound by boundaries of silver and gold

You were born to soar

BORN TO BE FREE

Because I kept in you a bit of me!

Prisoner of My Dreams

I had a dream, a grand vision, of which legends are made. The dream was so real that I could almost touch, smell and feel it. It was my destiny, the sole purpose for which I was born. It had to be, why else would I have this dream, day after day, night after night, every moment in my conscious and subconscious mind. It was only a matter of time. No matter where I went, what path I chose, the final destination was a foregone conclusion. At a very early age, God had given me a sneak-peek of my glorious future. Or was it? Was my dream really *my* dream? Were the visions really a sneak-peek from my benevolent almighty God or were they just fantasies of an innocent over-fertile mind. Maybe I had created these fantasies to run away from the prison of my mundane and perhaps painful reality. Well, the visions did take me away from the prison and gave me an alternative reality, a reality with the holy grail in my hand. And I perused that holy grail with all I had, knowing the universe conspires to bring to you what your heart truly desires.

But maybe desire is different from a dream. Maybe, in my effort to escape from one prison, I had created another prison for myself. I had wilfully become a slave to my dream. People, space, time, joy, sorrow, all blurred in my quest. Perhaps I was destined to only touch, feel, see but never 'have' the holy grail. As I look back, I see I sacrificed all my todays for that glorious tomorrow, and regardless of how far I've come, I still feel like a pauper with my hands empty.

Life is quite simple really. Know yourself and then try to be the best version of yourself. The problem arises when you start seeing yourself through other's eyes and then try to live up to their expectations. Sometimes your own vision of yourself is not 'yours'. It is what you were told when you were a child. 'This is good', 'this is bad', 'this is what makes you worthy', 'this is worth striving for'. 'Success' has played a very big role in my life. I have always heard two things in my life: 'you are so good' and 'you can do so much better'. On the surface these two statements are perfectly logical and perhaps appropriate and encouraging as well, but if you hear them often enough and start believing them, the two statements merge into one: 'you're not good enough'! So you spend your entire life trying to be better, to be 'good enough'. Even your 'success' is actually a 'failure' because you could have always done better.

And what is the barometer for 'better'? More often than not, it is recognition, money and sometimes happiness itself. When I look back, sure I have more money and recognition than before but what's the point, because all my mind tells me is 'you have so much further to go'. So before I can rejoice, there is always another mountain to climb. It's like you are always second best. Yes, you are getting 'better' but the glass will never be full, no matter how hard you try. Many a great have died a miserable unfulfilled sad life in spite of their brilliant body of work, compelled by their passion, running from their own shadow or maybe just trying in vain, to make that proverbial glass more than half full.

I live vicariously through the characters I perform. In reality I don't exist. Sometimes it feels like one is going round and round in a race, driven by a passion to excel, encouraged by the audience cheering you on, and all you're really doing is trying to outrun your own shadow and finally have a fleeting sense of joy and self-worth. After a while you question yourself. What am I doing? Is it really worth it? It's never been about 'competition' ... I see their eyes and the end line means something to them. I once was like that, but now I know the end line is just a matador's red cloth which will shift the moment you get close to it. Some say it's not reaching the end but the pursuit that's important. So we are all rats running round and round and we should be happy with that. The red ribbon at the 'end' means nothing, the track means nothing. But that's the only life I know, so I try to block the cheers, ignore the end line, stop trying to be the best that I can be, and just take one stride at a time. Looking out for lush-green meadows where I can just lie down and stare at the blue sky. Don't want to be a rat any more or run from my shadow, just want to dream another dream which will truly be mine.

Circle

ROUND AND ROUND AND ROUND I GO

Through the same places I've been before

The same highs, the same lows

The same uncertainties, the same unsures

Will I? Won't I? Can I? Can't I?

How many times the same fears must face I?

And will there be an end

Will there be some light?

Will there be a happy ending

to this dreary dark night?

In search of that pot of gold

at the end of the rainbow

Epilogue

WALK THE MIST

Searching for answers

Everywhere, except where lies the solution

The key lies on the other side of the mist

Through the unknown, the unsafe.

On the other side lies paradise

Clarity of purpose, potential of true self

And true happiness

In between lie your worst fears

The fear of loneliness

The fear of being alone

No one to love or be loved by

The fear of being inconsequential

The fear of simply withering away

Unnoticed, let alone mourned

Not belonging to anyone and no one belonging to you

No one in front, behind or beside

Only you and the rest of the world

Walking through the mist tears

Every pretence of the self
Until you are left alone, unsheltered, unclothed
Just the weak, timid, incomplete you
Yes, the mist is dark and dense
It is easier to run back to the security of the illusion
But beyond it is the paradise of your true perfect self.
Have to have courage
Have to walk the mist.